MATTERS
of the
Heart

MATTERS
of the
Heart

RUTH CHERRY, Ph.D.

ISBN: 979-8-89175-169-9 (sc)
ISBN: 979-8-89175-170-5 (e)

2025.01.21

Print information available on the last page.

This book is printed on acid-free paper.

Contents

For my clients who have been my best teachers

Chapter 1

GOOD PEOPLE

Like most of my clients, from some place way inside me, I've always longed to "be good." I've tried to figure out what the "right" thing in any given situation was and to do that. I've tried to be what I thought some authority wanted me to be.

Wanting to be good was a curse. Growing up in the sixties when the thing to do was be cool, wanting to be good insured that I would never be quite "with it." No one else seemed to be burdened with that curse. I watched other kids having fun, doing crazy spontaneous things, not thinking too much about what they "should" do – just enjoying themselves.

Like my sister. She was one year younger than I, and always, growing up, she looked to me like the epitome of cool. She was popular and had lots of friends, dates, and fun. She started trends while I couldn't even follow them. She knew all the cool words and styles while mostly I thought about how awkward I must look. She was extroverted while I have always been painfully introverted. Was anything hard for her?

The only thing that wasn't hard for me was making good grades which resulted in further isolation from the other kids. But making good grades was one way of being good and gaining loads of approval from my parents and teachers. Teachers always did think I was a good kid. I was sure I was doing what God wanted me to do when I got good grades. And I didn't have to work particularly hard for them. School was always an arena in which I could shine and experience success – sometimes the only arena.

The ultimate person to please was God. At the Catholic girls' school I attended, the structure for viewing reality was to follow God's rules as interpreted by the Sisters. Thus, it was ultimately pleasing to God if we were quiet when class started. God wanted me to avoid boys and to treat them as second class citizens if I ever had to speak to one of them. God didn't really like boys and didn't think too well of those people who did. So when I would snub Jimmy Thibadaux when he said hello, I knew I was pleasing God. If God were here, He would do the same thing. "Treat others as you want to be treated" did not include boys, who were the source of evil and should be punished for having the bad taste to be born male.

Of course, understanding that much about boys, sex didn't need to be mentioned. If God didn't want you to talk to boys, you didn't need to ask about doing anything else with them. They were not to be treated with kindness.

Therefore, the implication was that I would be a better person and would be good in God's eyes if I were not sexual and didn't have sexual thoughts, feelings, or interests. I didn't decide any of that consciously. My choice was so subtle and so deep that, without knowing it, the sexual part of me ceased to exist. And that was before it had really been born. I never really had any sexual feelings or any physical desires. I did notice many years later that puberty was when I first started gaining weight and that around the time of my period, my appetite was insatiable.

Eating too much or not exercising enough was never a sin or even a little bit wrong. If one were intellectual, the condition of the body was unimportant. In fact, being concerned about the body at all was discouraged. Having a body was one of the burdens related to being human and being relieved of that burden at death was definitely something to anticipate. Meanwhile one should focus on developing a keen intellect and being as close to a pure spirit as possible.

The amount of time kneeling in Church was indicative of the disrespect the Catholic Church in the 50's and 60's seemed to have for bodies. Kneeling without resting one's derriere on the seat and keeping one's elbows off the railing was a discipline for the "weak body." If it pained a body, it was good. The discipline would get a body into line. With enough aching and with constant descipline, the spirit would learn to rise above the body and one would somehow end a better person than one began.

Saying "No" when the body said, "I'm uncomfortable and I'd like to move," would probably make God happy. If the body suffered, God was pleased. "No" was His favorite word.

God was a "He" in those days. Religion was a matter of denial and control, fraught with threats of punishment to be delivered by an angry, condemning male. Being good equalled always following the rules.

Discipline was a good way of silencing any voice that arose from inside. The inside of the body was not to be trusted but to be disciplined and brought into line with the intellect, with doing what one "should." Nothing that would arise from inside my body – impulses, wishes, feelings, or fantasies – would please God. God wanted a little nun – quiet, robot-like, doing things "perfectly."

The part of me that told me how I should be, my Controller, became obsessed with being perfect. Perfect meant having a non-threatening facade, fitting in, and not making waves. Don't rock the boat. Be nice. Don't make anyone uncomfortable. Give people what they want. Be a pleaser. Don't think about your own wants.

By the time I was an adult I had an overdeveloped Controller and a puny Child. Their conversations went like this:

Controller: You have to be productive. Do more, read more, and definitely think more. You're far too emotional with all those amorphous feelings. Yech!

Get it together!! Set your goals, work toward them, and don't lose sight of where you want to be tomorrow. Forget today. Plan for tomorrow.

To which my Child replied:

Child: Yes, ma'am.

I'm horrified to admit it but that's the truth. My Child swallowed every word my Controller said unquestioningly and did her best to fit an inflexible mold. My Controller cut off my Child's wants so well.

My Controller told her, You should be more intellectual. (My Child was pretty mushy, I admit it.) You need to work very, very hard or else (who-knows-what) tragic consequences will ensue. (The Controller never specified the feared outcome but it was something equivalent to death or eternal damnation or being publicly embarrassed forever.)

And my Controller would continue:

Don't be needy and don't look needy. Just don't need. Not anything. Not anyone. Never. My Child tried hard to adhere to these strictures. She didn't protest, didn't complain. She never even felt mistreated by this Controller. She knew it was all for her best and that sometime in the future she'd be rewarded. So she acquiesced to the point of almost disappearing.

And over the years I acquired some degrees and licenses and a modicum of respectability. But inside I wasn't comfortable. I didn't hear from my Child too loudly but as an adult I did notice a pattern among my clients.

The clients I talk with describe their life choices and decisions couched in a context of wanting to do the "right" thing. Each one is concerned with acting appropriately, being a participating member of society and doing her job well. Each one cares about making her life good and her relationships satisfying. They want to give and receive love and hope that someday they will feel comfortable and enjoy being alive.

When it is time to make a decision or to act my clients take their responsibilities seriously. Each thinks about what she has been taught is right by an authority. The outer authority had credibilty and the child trusted what she was told. Now as an adult in conflict, her first point of reference is someone or something from the past, a former authority now alive in her head. She recalls something she has been taught and applies that to her current situation. Now she is "good," doing what she believes is expected of her. ("I won't say anything. I don't want to make things worse.")

These decisions often result in continued pain for the client. The hope that her perseverance will finally result in situational change is often frustrated. Seldom are the rewards she expected for being good forthcoming. Life doesn't become easier, other people don't respect her more, and relationships don't flourish. ("Doesn't anyone understand?! Why won't they help me?")

Each client knows her own rules for being good and follows them, but her expectations about receiving protection from unhappiness as a reward for her efforts are unfulfilled. In fact, these good people often hurt more, feel increased frustration and disappointment, and seem to be further from their goals of peace and happiness than ever.

This process reinforces the client's perception of herself as a powerless Child and someone else (parents, teachers, God) as a powerful authority. The authority has all the answers about how to make life work smoothly and the child has to guess the behavior expected of her in order to be taken protected by the authority. ("I couldn't possibly say what I really feel. They'd throw me out on my ear and I don't know how I would survive.")

By identifying with the powerless Child in themselves, these clients repeatedly guess answers which prolong their own pain but which they hope make them good. ("I know he'll quit drinking if I just hang in there.") Fear is at the basis of their choices. They are suffering but fear the possible consequences of changing.

Perhaps always volunteering to chauffeur the school children is draining and frustrating but these clients don't refuse. Living with a selfish demanding husband may be depleting, but good clients always take care of him.

While growing up these good people didn't trust the voice which came from their own feelings or wants, but they did have another voice strongly implanted in their heads which was louder and demanded their compliance. Originally this voice came from a feared/revered authority but now the voice lives in their heads. Even when they are alone they hear clearly and loudly just what the Authority expects.

That voice now has its own life within them. Other inner voices, the ones that are needy or wanting or scared, are silenced in deference to this now internalized Authority. They believe the Authority voice will lead them to safety and fulfillment while their wanting and needing voices will only lead them to danger. Thus, these good people opt out of their own feelings and side with an external Authority, now living inside them.

Eventually these good people did not know when they felt fear or anger or fatigue or jealousy. They had lost connection to their inner worlds. Any inner voices which did not comply with the Authority's expectations were silenced. Without knowing it they decided that if they can't "solve" their problems in the outer world, they just won't have the feelings that "cause" so many problems. ("Everyone has hard times. No one wants to hear about my disappointment. I'll just get on with life.")

Needing to be self-reliant and in control means that they don't share their hurts and frustrations with another who might listen and sympathize and possibly offer another point of view. Instead, they learn well to carry their suffering by themselves accepting emotional isolation from others and from their own feelings. They side with the world outside (now very well re-created in their heads) which tells them to ignore their feelings. They learn their roles well – whether at work or at home – about how they "should" behave. They fit in. They look just fine. (Except for the obesity or the compulsive dieting or the obsessive busyness.)

When Good People hurt we say to ourselves, "Be quiet. Make other people comfortable." When we are angry we say, "Don't make waves; do it their way." When we are needy we say "Think of all the folks who really have it bad. Don't be selfish." We have a silencing response for whatever voice arises within us.

After listening only to the Authority telling us what to do we develop insomnia, arthritis, migraines, constipation, colitis, or obesity. And we may or may not put it all together that listening to that internalized Authority while ignoring our inner feeling voices, results in physical pain. After all, who would think that just trying to be good would hurt your body?

Sound familiar? If you have ever thought in any of these ways or drawn any of these conclusions, I'd like to share my observations and experiences with you. Life hasn't been easy for me and while I might like to point my finger at someone and say, "It's your fault; if you hadn't been around, I would have been happy," I know in my heart and soul that I can't avoid taking responsibility for myself. Blaming is a way of saying, "I don't .want to look inside me to understand how I am creating my own reality."

There is an undeniable correlation between our choices to ignore parts of our inner worlds and our outer world experiences. If I disown some of my feelings, I will still see them but now they will look like they come from outside me. It will appear that my husband is not sensitive to my feelings. In fact, he is just saying aloud what an inner subpersonality of mine is already communicating – "I really am not interested."

Healing occurs when conflicts are resolved on an unconscious level. Healing demands that we re-own and integrate those parts of ourselves which have been alienated. Our loyalty shifts from that Authority's voice that booms in our heads to the subtle whispers we can barely discern in our hearts.

When we are willing to accept responsibility for our inner worlds we can know who is alive and operating in there. We are all more comfortable with some parts of ourselves than with others but whatever subpersonalities live inside us are ours to know and to heal. So, when we want to acknowledge *what is*, we surrender and allow our inner worlds to guide us.

To begin this process, do the following relaxation exercise. You may want to record these instructions so that you can listen to them passively with your eyes closed. Or, if you prefer, have a friend read them to you.

RELAXATION EXERCISE

Be comfortable. (Pause for ten seconds.) When you are ready allow your eyes to close. (pause) For a few minutes follow your breathing, watching the air as it comes in and goes out of your body. (pause) Let your mind release the busyness of the day and allow your tension to gently float away. (pause) Focus your attention on your breathing. Allow any thoughts to just pass through your mind as though they were dancers on a stage, entering from the left and leaving to the right. (pause) Follow your inhales and your exhales and allow your breath to carry you deeper within yourself. (pause) Notice a slight letting go in your muscles and allow your body to relax as much as it's willing to. (pause)

As you are drawn deeper within, release the outer world and let it fade away. (pause) All of your attention is focused on your inner world. (pause) Let your breath carry you out of your head, down into your body, and notice what it's like to be in your body right now. (pause) Continue to follow your breathing and allow yourself to be pulled deeper within.

REFLECTIONS

In a spiral notebook or on a piece of paper, write your reactions to doing the Relaxation Exercise.

Did feelings come up that surprised you? Did some thoughts occur that you weren't expecting? Was there anything you said to yourself?

How easy is it to relax? What inside your head makes it hard to relax? What's dangerous about relaxing?

Could you hear more clearly from a deeper level in you? What do you want from this level?

Chapter 2

KNOWING YOUR OWN SHADOW

"Unconscious" is a scary word because who knows what it means? You can't see it, it's not the same for everyone, and it challenges definition. So, why bother? Maybe it doesn't really exist. Maybe we can just plug along doing what seems reasonable and life will turn out fine.

Actually, that approach works adequately. For a while. But for each of us there comes a time when we realize that something other than our conscious minds is at play in our lives. Something we have not chosen and something which isn't very comfortable. What we would like to be and to present to the world is not really the essence of who we are. Regardless of our conscious choices, there is a part of ourselves we cannot control and direct.

A very, very large part of each of us is not intellectual or focused or self-willed. And after a few months or years of being frustrated, unsatisfied, confused, and, maybe, in pain, we realize that there is a pattern to the situations in which we find ourselves stuck. When our problems come up they are uncannily similar to the problems we had last year and ten years ago and twenty years ago.

Alone in the darkness of our own rooms, we suspect that something in <u>us</u> is creating this pattern. We have ignored it as long as we can but finally this discomfort has become unbearable and we have exhausted our rational resources. We scream "Uncle" then we look inside.

At this point we acknowledge our unconscious Shadow – the storehouse for all those facets of ourselves which we have rejected, which we feared would lead us into danger, and which we hid from others. We probably adopted a role we could play instead of being ourselves. Identifying with the Hard Worker or the Compliant Companion or the Gifted Child enabled us to pretend that our enraged Teenager or our selfish Prima Donna didn't exist. By playing a role we could ignore those unpleasant aspects of ourselves as well as hide them from others. For awhile. But in the end acting a role doesn't make life turn out right, save us from disappointment, or make our struggles disappear.

And we realize that we can't escape dealing with our own hidden monsters. The anger we tried to kill when we were four didn't die but has lived, hidden but growing, in the dark places inside us. The vulnerability we tried so hard to deny by achieving competence in the adult world still exists. That little Child in so much pain is still in us, waiting to be picked up. We hoped she was gone but she's still there and now she won't let us walk away.

So, defeated in our hopes of constructing an outer life separate from the one inside, we sit down and look into ourselves. And we <u>have</u> to acknowledge our unconscious. Because we would never <u>choose</u> what we find when we look inside, we know something else is operating. Reluctantly we agree to acquaint ourselves with this unconscious Shadow which is so powerful in our lives and so specifically personal.

One way to comprehend the workings of the unconscious inner world is to think in terms of subpersonalities. Subpersonalities do not indicate a split personality or psychosis. Subpersonalities are the different parts of ourselves. We've always known about subpersonalities, we've just called them moods or roles or monsters. "I don't know what happened. Something inside me made me quit my job and give away all my belongings and move across the country. What was I thinking of?" Or, "I don't know why. I never act like that but I knew I had to meet him. So I walked up and introduced myself and started talking. I would never do that again."

The fact that we can identify different parts of ourselves and feel the tension between them is a sign of health. Flexibility is the goal; we want to be able to move among our subpersonalities as needed. We have many subpersonalities. Over time new ones emerge and familiar ones mature. Our inner world is always in flux.

Recently, I was preparing a seminar and I realized that I needed to listen to my subpersonalities. I knew someone inside had something to say because I was feeling anxious. First I heard from my Wimp. She's a young, emaciated woman wearing a dowdy print dress that hangs from her bony shoulders. She said, "You can't do this presentation. You have nothing to offer. They'll hate you. It will all be terrible and you'll be humiliated." She offered these comments in a whining voice, a bit hysterically. Within a few minutes I heard from another female voice, the Hard Worker. About 50, with broad shoulders and a torso that was solid and unbudgeable, she said, "Don't give in to that hysteria. Just look through every book on your bookshelf and gather all the information you need from what others have written. Compile their quotes and build a presentation from that."

I followed the Hard Worker's direction but after an hour I felt frustrated and fatigued. Fatigue is another way I can tell I need to listen to some part inside me. It indicates to me that one part has been dominant too long and others haven't been heard. When I sat back, I heard from my long suffering, stringy haired female Masochist. She said, "Go ahead and suffer. It's only five more weeks. You can enjoy yourself later. Just forget about having any fun next month." I found that depressing and went to bed.

The next morning, feeling refreshed, I first heard from my Playful Child, an eight-year-old boy dressed in navy blue shorts, a red tee shirt, and a dark baseball cap. He said that he wanted to have fun and he wanted the seminar to be fun.

Several minutes later I heard from the Creative Adult. This was another masculine voice, about thirty-four who wore a loose shirt in a deep shade of green. He said, "Don't worry about breaking your back to get a lot of work done. Just allow it to come from inside you." He told me that I already knew everything I needed and to pull the words from within me instead of gathering data from outside me.

Over the next week these five parts met together. I watched as the Creative Adult emerged as the leader of the group. He talked with each subpersonality individually until they agreed on the contribution each would make to the presentation. To the Wimp he said, "I appreciate your awareness that this seminar will take some preparation. You have reminded us that we can't put off thought about this project until the night before. Please keep reminding us every few days that we need to be ready physically by eating well, sleeping adequately, and exercising. And please insure that the right clothes are ready."

To the Hard Worker he said, "I appreciate your sense of responsibility. I need you to make sure that the car is running well, that there is enough gas, and that you have directions to the location." The Hard Worker agreed and diligently assumed her duties. To the Masochist the Creative Adult said, "I appreciate your ability to persist. Please help us work consistently and evenly, not overdoing or forgetting. Sure and steady." She nodded and seriously contemplated her task.

And to the Playful Child he smiled and said, "I appreciate your enthusiasm. Please share that with our group. That would be a welcome contribution." The Playful Child beamed, glad to be acknowledged. As for himself, the Creative Adult said that he would be responsible for the content of the presentation. He would create a seminar from his imagination and experience.

Each part agreed to do his or her appropriate task. I certainly didn't want the Masochist to be responsible for the content of the presentation or the Playful Child to be in charge of getting the car ready. Each subpersonality was satisfied to do a job appropriate for his or her talents.

We get into trouble when we expect one subpersonality to do a job which fits another subpersonality. When it's time to play, we need a Playful Child, and when it's time to work we need a Responsible Adult. We also get into trouble when we give one subpersonality an inordinate amount of time and energy. If the Hard Worker is dominant ninety percent of the time, the other subpersonalities will feel stifled. If one subpersonality is disproportionately large, we are expending our energy in an imbalanced way.

For those of us super-responsible Good People, there is an imbalance in the time and energy we divide among our subpersonalities. We favor the duty oriented figures and neglect the more spontaneous ones. Consequently, we have too many headaches and too much gastrointestinal disorder; we grind our teeth too frequently and the insomnia is draining. Someone is pressing for recognition through all these symptoms and now we must listen. We need to discover who is there and what s/he wants.

When I work with clients the first thing I do is listen to the different subpersonalities as the client talks. In that way, we can define the conflicts and identify the unconscious beliefs aligned with each subpersonality underlying the client's experience. To say:

"My Rebellious Teenager is angry and refuses to cooperate with my Controller" describes the client's internal experience of always being late even though she says she wants to arrive on time. She owns and respects both parts of herself and takes responsibility for the conflict being internal.

Differentiating the parts of ourselves, owning each one, and speaking clearly for them is like turning on a light in that dark inner world. We can then recognize that the feelings of the Scared Infant ("I'm so scared to be alone. I need someone to love and protect me.") are different from the desires of the Loser ("Who cares anyway. I'll never get a promotion. Why even try?")or the needs of the independence-seeking Adolescent ("Don't tell me how you do it. I'm not you. Watch and learn how I do it.")

When we can identify our inner world experience specifically by putting the words with the particular subpersonality who utter them, we realize that we are not crazy or insatiably needy. When we feel hysterical or mixed-up it's just two or three subpersonalities whose voices have become tangled. We can clarify our inner world jumble by listening to and knowing each subpersonality. The forces at work in our inner worlds are identifiable and, more important, ready to be healed. Our subpersonalities want to be known and heard.

Just like children, the subpersonalities in us change and grow. As their needs are met, they move into a new fuller way of being. All they need in order to mature is to be accepted and acknowledged. When we give them what they need, they continue on their growing-up path.

It's when they haven't received what they need that they remain stuck. It's then that they need to be listened to. Our inner worlds have their own schedule and standards and logic. They operate consistently and make sense in their own terms. When we learn to speak to and listen to the unconscious we can know our inner worlds.

Do you doubt this process? Skepticism is normal; it will not diminish the efficacy of the exercises. Do the following exercise (or another from this book) daily and write your experience. See if you notice patterns in your inner world. See what patterns occur in your outer world experience. Notice what happens when you make a commitment to know and accept your inner life.

The first step in this process of knowing your inner world is to listen. Shift your focus inside and temprarily disregard the outer world with all its activity and distraction.

EXERCISE

Do the Relaxation Exercise from page 9.

And then follow it with this imagery exercise:

Breathe and move your attention inside. Let your breath carry your attention from your head down into your body. (pause) Notice how easy it is to breathe. You don't have to think about breathing or try to breathe. You just breathe. (pause) All your attention is focused inside your body. If thoughts run through your head, that's fine. You just don't have to pay attention to them now. Watch your inbreaths and your outbreaths. (pause)

Your breath carries your attention to a spot in the center of your body. (pause) Your mind doesn't have to know where this spot is, your breath will carry you there. (pause) Breathe into that spot and focus your attention right there. (pause) Then your breath carries you through that spot. You find yourself in a small clearing with a semi-circle of trees bordering it. Focus on the clearing and breathe. (pause)

From the trees a figure walks into the clearing. Just watch. (pause) What do you notice about this figure. It may be human, animal, inanimate. Notice the details of this figure. (pause) Notice what the figure is doing. (pause) If you don't know which part of you this figure represents, ask. Listen to what it tells you. (pause)

There is some message that this figure wants to give you. Listen receptively. You don't need your mind. (pause) What do you hear? Be still and feel this message in your body. (pause) Ask the figure if it has anything else which you need to hear. (pause)

Ask the figure anything you want to and listen. (pause) When you have no more questions, thank the figure, assure it you will return, and let your imagery fade. (pause)

REFLECTIONS

Write about your imagery exerience. Describe the figure and what it said to you.

What part of you is it? What was surprising about this figure? What was familiar?

Do you trust what you were given? What does your mind say to you to limit your trust?

Your unconscious communicates with you in pictures. What did you learn about your inner world from seeing the images?

Write any associations you have to what you have just experienced. How is this figure now involved in your daily life? How could it possibly be involved in the future?

Call on this figure once or twice this week and ask it for its suggestions about handling whatever is going on inside you or outside you.

Chapter 3

THE CONTROL/ COMPLIANCE GAME

Wednesdays are quiet at the office; that's why I like them. Most of the other six therapists take the day off and leave their offices empty. Only Karen, whose office is in the corner, and I share the waiting room. I've scheduled most of my work for Wednesdays. I turn down the radio and close the outside door so there is no noise intruding into my small private space.

I especially enjoy my time with my two o'clock client. Kate is forty-five and originally came into my office saying that she needed help letting go of her children. With her wavy red hair, hazel eyes, and alabaster skin, she sat alertly, not leaning against the back of the chair. She was neat and well groomed, conservative in her dark shirtwaist and black pumps. No one could criticize her appearance unless it was for lack of flourish. By looking at her, I knew nothing about Kate except her preference for the traditionally acceptable. She did not seem like a risk taker.

Kate's sons were in their early twenties and had recently left home for graduate school. She sensed that her work in life would never be the same. For over twenty years Kate had listened to and nurtured her family, creating an ambience of warmth and support in their home. She had decorated and cooked and sewn and had truly enjoyed herself. She was very proud of both her sons. She had loved her role of nurturing mother and found great satisfaction in it.

Kate described her relationship with Dan, her husband of twenty-five years, as unusually harmonious. They had always been especially close, sensing a tie she described as "lasting through many lifetimes." They had known each other from childhood. They seldom argued and seemed to find an ongoing sense of appreciation and pleasure in each other's company.

Recently, however, Kate's three family relationships had changed. Her children no longer needed her attention. In universities across the country, they were caught up in their own busy lives. Dan admitted that he was restless and was feeling his own shifts. He did not respond to Kate as compliantly as he had in the past. There were parts of him that pressed for greater expression and independence and he had to listen to them, he said.

Kate didn't resent these changes but was left feeling confused and unsure about herself. What was her role now? And what would be her consuming work? She had always defined herself in terms of mother and wife. Now it was time to "be" differently and she had no idea what that meant. She felt like she had lost everything she loved, everything that had focused her time and energy, even her thinking. A huge part of her life had ended abruptly and she was in mourning.

During our first meeting, Kate was pleasant but cried intermittently while we talked. Her feelings were surprising to her and overwhelming. "After all, Dan and I have raised our boys to be successful. Now they are. And, believe me, I wouldn't have it any other way. Why do I feel so lost?" Now she had exactly what she had wanted for two decades – for her sons to be independent and self-motivated – and she was miserable. "Am I crazy? My friends say we have the perfect family. I used to think so but now I don't know what is happening. If only I understood," and she sighed as she dabbed the tears overflowing her eyes. Her feelings were mystifying and not explainable solely from the loss of her sons. Something else was happening in her that she couldn't fathom or change or even define.

At the end of our session, I realized that I had been touched by the depth of Kate's pain and by her confusion. "How can I be so unhappy," she said, "when I've always done everything I thought was right and when everything has turned out so well? I'm not unhappy about anything that has happened. I'm just so . . . Oh, I don't know. I just don't understand." And she put her head in her hands.

This woman who had been so put together at the beginning of our session, now, at the end, realized that it wasn't her outer world, which she had always handled deftly, which was troublesome, but her inner world which she had never really thought about before. Something new was demanded from inside her but that inside world was unknown territory.

At our second session I suggested that we do some imagery work. I surprised myself by doing this. Usually I wait several sessions until I sense that a trusting relationship has developed between the client and me. An unconscious part of me must have known that Kate would receive this suggestion openly.

As I mentioned imagery, Kate's face brightened. She told me about a class that she and Dan had taken the previous year. They had learned that their imagery was spontaneous – totally separate from and independent of their conscious minds, arising from a source deep within them. In the class they had learned to passively respect the integrity of their imagery, watching their mental pictures move and change without any direction from their minds or from the leader. Because of this prior experience Kate was already comfortable with her imagery.

In my work with clients I don't usually explain imagery work in theoretical terms. I just say that we have all the wisdom we need inside ourselves, in our unconscious. Imagery is the language of the unconscious. It shows us our own truths. So, if there are apparent obstacles in our everyday conscious worlds – we find ourselves repeating self sabotaging patterns or we feel frustrated and unclear about what to do next – we can find the resources we need to move ahead by going inside to the unconscious.

When I do imagery work with clients we both close our eyes and then I lead them into a state of relaxation for several minutes. We concentrate on watching the breath and allow our muscles to relax. We enter a realm of deeper awareness in which the outer reality fades and is no longer the focus of attention. We move into the inner world where a different way of perceiving is called forth.

By walking with Kate through her imagery, I know I will gain a glimpse of her inner world. I allow my mind to become blank and I follow her lead. I have no sense of where we are going or what we will encounter. I don't want to choreograph her imagery journey; my role is to facilitate her awareness of her own unconscious. I know that her unconscious will guide us in the direction of growth and wholeness. I also know that neither my mind nor Kate's mind nor any other conscious intellectual process could be as accurate or as effective as her unconscious.

I have learned through my own experience that we can trust the unconscious. If we can understand its language – imagery – we can decipher its messages. The unconscious message is unfailing in offering the precise guidance that's needed at the moment.

Our unconscious imagery portrays our subpersonalities, the many different energies within us. For example, we may have a part which pushes us to achieve and acquire professional respectability – the Driver. The Driver may exhort us not to rest, demanding that we work toward our goals constantly. And in our imagery the Driver may appear as a bulldozer or a visored bookkeeper.

On Saturday afternoons, we may notice the prominence of the Lazy Layabout. Perhaps that figure appears to us as our older brother asleep on the couch in front of the televised football game. (Even though we may recognize the face of someone else, it is still our subpersonality.) And by Saturday night, another subpersonality has taken control of most of our energy, perhaps the Party Animal (a fraternity man in a blue blazer with gold buttons) or the Flirt (a young woman in a slinky black evening dress). One way to know the unconscious is to know the different subpersonalities operating within us. The forms their images take are unlimited and can be human, animal, or inanimate. Anything goes with the unconscious.

Kate and I close our eyes, breathe, and turn our attention inward. I coach Kate by saying, "Wait and listen. A figure inside you will appear to you. He or she has something to give you. Wait receptively. When an image becomes clear to you, describe it to me." Because of Kate's earlier experience with imagery, she can easily focus her attention within herself expectantly and "look" at the products of her unconscious.

As Kate realizes which figure is coming to her, she describes that figure's appearance and behavior. She sees the image unfold as she describes it to me with her eyes closed. Sometimes she laughs or cries as the figure says something to her. It is a revelation for her, as though she is watching a play she has no part in producing. In fact, her unconscious is delivering the images to her and her conscious mind simply receives them.

One of the first parts of Kate whom we met was a very young playful male – the Little Rascal. (His name "came" to her as his image appeared.) This freckle-faced six-year-old was full of fun. In his jeans, rolled up at the ankles, he would hide and climb trees and play pranks. There was nothing serious about him.

Kate's ability to relax her intellectual control enough to hear from and see her inner figures is a sign of strength. She is comfortable acknowledging her inner world within the context of therapy. She doesn't feel overrun by it or afraid.

As Kate watched the Little Rascal (and often laughed), she learned that he was not intimidated by anyone. Not even by the second subpersonality we met – the Judge. This large stern woman sitting behind a huge desk gave Kate her "shoulds." "You should be pleasant. Nobody likes a sad sack." And "You should be more patient. Think of Saint Theresa." And sometimes, "You really should be doing more. You have the time now."

Almost every session we encountered this six-foot tall, heavy Judge with her brown hair in a bun. Kate said of the Judge's appearance, "She scowls so that her heavy eyebrows almost touch." And Kate shivered.

After recognizing her feelings when the Judge spoke – intimidation and fear – Kate realized that the Judge's influence was with her much of the time. She often felt afraid and intimidated. Although she was not comfortable with the Judge, Kate could identify the Judge in her. When she heard herself saying "should" or "ought" or "I really must do this," she knew it was the Judge speaking.

The Judge would reprimand the Little Rascal: "That's <u>not</u> OK!" Or give him a job to do: "Get the garage organized and do it today!" "What's the difference," the Little Rascal would interject into a very serious Judge speech, "between an elephant and a cup of coffee?" Of course, the Judge would be stymied, stop mid-sentence, and stare at him blankly.

"Oh, no," he'd continue, "we're in trouble if you can't tell those two apart!" And he would roar.

After several weeks, Kate could say that the Little Rascal offered her a reprieve from the pounding of the Judge's constant injunctions. When Kate took herself too seriously (identified with the Judge), the Little Rascal made fun of her – "Guess you're not ready to be canonized yet!" When she was burdened by responsibilities, he would laugh. "What, is the back giving out? Try bending the knees. You'll be able to carry more then." The Little Rascal was gentle in his teasing and always showed Kate a creative way of viewing herself. He added humor and often reminded her, "Practice, practice, practice enjoying yourself." "A breath of fresh air," Kate would say shaking her head in appreciation. The Little Rascal didn't loosen up the Judge but the Judge didn't cramp him, either.

Kate also met a Reader, a female figure about sixteen who was quiet and didn't interact with anyone. Mostly, she stayed by herself and read. She didn't want to make trouble. This girl looked plain, kept her eyes down, and didn't speak. Kate knew the Reader by the feeling that filled her when she saw the Reader – shame.

The Reader was closely related to a figure we soon learned was prominent with Kate, the Dutiful Daughter. Kate imaged the Dutiful Daughter as a slender, twenty-year-old woman with long straight light brown hair. She was timid and self-effacing. The Dutiful Daughter wanted the approval of everyone, particularly the Judge. The Dutiful Daughter decided what she would do based upon knowing what the Judge expected of her. Just as the Little Rascal was all spontaneity, the Dutiful Daughter had no spontaneity, only duty. She seemed to view herself as powerless and her only job as pleasing the Judge. "Yes'm," she would say as she bowed her head.

Kate soon realized that much of the time she was identified with the Dutiful Daughter. She reacted to others and spoke in the same manner that the Dutiful Daughter spoke. In her Dutiful Daughter, Kate was compliant, ready to serve, and focused on the Judge's demands. By identifying with the Dutiful Daughter, Kate blocked her spontaneity (the Little Rascal contained all of that) and her own authority over herself (the Dutiful Daughter was focused on the Judge's authority). She strove to accomplish the impossible goal of making the Judge happy. And that's how Kate lived most of her days – in her Dutiful Daughter subpersonality reacting to the Judge.

By identifying with the Dutiful Daughter, Kate was chronically fearful and frustrated. She was aware of the tension – of wanting to please and the anxiety which arose from her fear that she wasn't acceptable to the Judge.

Kate could describe well her Dutiful Daughter's efforts at service. She consciously owned that part of her. She truly liked being "helpful." But the Judge was a subpersonality with whom Kate was not so consciously identified. Although she generally did not present herself to others as a Judge, the Judge aspect of Kate was evident to her family. They were familiar with her subtle criticisms about what was not OK and her pursed lips when she was dissatisfied. They could read the anger in her raised eyebrows and averted eyes. Kate didn't want to see her own rigidity and didn't want to be seen by others as "controlling." She found these qualities distasteful and, so, she denied having them. This refusal to become conscious of the Judge part of her only fueled that part, giving it power and influence. Inevitably its judgment and impatience crept into her interactions.

On a very subtle level (not even in Kate's awareness), the Dutiful Daughter understood the Judge's commands and immediately tensed to respond to them. Kate was aware of her tension but because she was not well acquainted with the Judge, she didn't identify with being the Judge who caused the Dutiful Daughter pain. She only identified with being the recipient of that pain. In the Judge/Dutiful Daughter polarity, Kate owned the Dutiful Daughter qualities consciously and expressed the Judge qualities unconsciously. Thus, the relationship between these two figures was maintained.

Kate also recognized another subpersonality whom she called Mark Twain. He was especially good at giving Kate advice about being grounded and stable. He had common sense and was reasonable. He had no need to please and didn't acknowledge any other subpersonality as having authority over him. His frequent statement to Kate was "Trust yourself." This subpersonality represented a Confident Adult part of Kate.

Obviously, Mark Twain wasn't a subpersonality with whom Kate identified easily as she did with the Dutiful Daughter. Over time, she came to learn that he was an available resource within her whom she could trust. When she contacted Mark he responded; he never imposed himself on her. His wisdom was subtle, but Kate recognized his fairness and his integrity. She felt confident when she heard from him.

By watching, listening to, and questioning her inner subpersonalities for several months, Kate learned that she was tyrannically ruled by the Judge who would never be satisfied. She saw that she was usually trapped by her identification with the Dutiful Daughter, who wold never stop trying to please the Judge. Into these scenes of female figures she might introduce the masculine flavor of Mark Twain or the Little Rascal. If the Dutiful Daughter, dejected by the Judge's inaccessibility was pouting, I might suggest to Kate, "See Mark Twain magically appear out of the shadows. He has a message for the Dutiful Daughter. Listen. Hear what he says to her." After a silent minute Kate would smile, her shoulders drop, and she would say, "Mark says, 'Not to worry.' I should plan a picnic for tomorrow and try a new recipe tonight. There are lots of other things I can think about."

In another session I might say, "Let's see what the Little Rascal would do in this scene. Notice him entering the picture and tell me what happens." And with a laugh Kate would describe the Little Rascal somersaulting over the Judge's desk and leaping to the floor with outstretched arms and a self-congratulatory "Ta Da!" She couldn't stay too somber when the little Rascal was around.

The Little Rascal added humor and Mark Twain added detachment. Just by the introduction of these two masculine figures, the tone of many of the discussions between the Dutiful Daughter and the Judge shifted. Kate imaged the feminine figures to have characteristics which were closer to her awareness – compliance, orderliness, and respect for others. Her masculine figures owned those characteristics which Kate hadn't yet integrated into her daily way of being – self-confidence, assertiveness, playfulness, and independence. All of her subpersonalities belonged to her; some were just easier for Kate to know.

Kate could consciously say she wanted to be liked (Dutiful Daughter). After much hard work in therapy, she realized that she (the Judge) was pressuring herself (the Dutiful Daughter) to meet traditional cultural expectations to earn approval. When she could laugh at herself (Little Rascal) for taking these "shoulds" (the Judge) so seriously, she could view her choices objectively (Mark Twain). Thus, her subpersonalities balanced each other.

With these resources, Kate could come to a temporary resolution of her discomfort during our sessions. But Kate's Judge had a very, very strong grip on her and asserted itself frequently in ways which crippled her. During one imagery session Kate focused on her body experience and spontaneously visualized a fist grabbing her chest and squeezing, trying to cut off her breath. It seemed to try to break her resistance to its control when it tightened her shoulders. Kate realized that the fist was her Judge's. When she described the Judge, her voice became softer as though she were intimidated by an external threatening figure. Her fear of the Judge's control was deep. Barely above a whisper Kate would say, "She's quite displeased with me now."

Several times Kate mentioned the word "power" as describing personal effectiveness. She quickly admitted that she was afraid of her own power. She knew the Judge did not want her (the Dutiful Daughter) to own her power and also realized that the Dutiful Daughter resisted being powerful. When we spoke before the imagery sessions, she would express (the Dutiful Daughter's) fear that owning her power and acting powerfully would alienate others from her and would deprive her of love. The Judge told Kate adamantly that if she relinquished a pleasing facade, no one would want to be around her. The Dutiful Daughter believed this statement completely.

All her life Kate had acted accordingly. She was a Peacemaker in groups and a Reliable Worker on the job. She and Dan had taught their children not to intrude on others and never to be resented. This was certainly Kate's rule for herself. "Be nice" was her motto.

As she told me about her self-imposed rules, she expressed no conflict. "I was raised to be a good Catholic girl," she said and she was consciously maintaining that role even now in middle age. She expected others to notice and to appreciate her for it. If she were not adequately appreciated, she felt resentful and used, but she didn't change her behavior. Not in public. Only the three people in her family saw her Shadow side, that darker arena where she shoved her anger and her power and her assertion – the parts of her she didn't like or trust but couldn't eradicate.

The Shadow is the unconscious receptacle for those parts of us we deem "unacceptable." Kate's Shadow received any characteristic her Judge condemned. Since her Dutiful Daughter was obedient, her Shadow contained her rebellion. Her Dutiful Daughter was sweet but her Shadow housed her rage. Kate's controlling Judge didn't want Kate to acknowledge her assertion so that went into her Shadow, also.

Kate reported difficulty sleeping and severe tension headaches at times. When I suggested that there might be a correlation between her identification with the Dutiful Daughter (and consequent refusal to see her Shadow qualities of anger, rebellion, and assertion) and these physical complaints, she became very innocent and unreflective. "Oh, well, lots of people have trouble. I can live with it." This willingness to tolerate suffering was preferable to realizing that she wasn't innocent, that she did have a dark side, and that there existed within her feelings which didn't fit "a good Catholic girl" image.

Kate had lived according to the Judge's commands, identified with the Dutiful Daughter, and stored her unacceptable feelings and subpersonalities in her Shadow all of her life. But subpersonalities can't be ignored without consequences ensuing. As her time to be a nurturing mother passed, there were no distractions from the undercover conflicts raging within her. Her anger, her unmet needs for relaxation, and her growing need to express herself all were strong. She wasn't a child any longer (and, therefore, unaware of her feelings or sincerely innocent) and she couldn't assume a role (Nurturing Mother) to avoid her tumultuous inner world. Her Judge had demanded for years that she not listen to other parts of herself. Now all those voices inside her thundered their demand that Kate acknowledge them.

As Kate's inner turmoil grew, she couldn't ignore the issue of power any longer. We discussed personal power as being the openness to hear from any voice within her at any time. Owning her power meant recognizing every subpersonality within her every time it wanted to speak. Quite a shift from aligning only with the Judge/Dutiful Daughter continuum and not one Kate would choose if she could avoid it. But over time our Shadows have a way of making themselves felt more and more insistently and Kate's time had come.

Kate opened one session by suggesting that there were additional subpersonalities inside her she probably didn't know. "Why aren't I taking more risks?" she questioned. "And why aren't I more of a leader? I have good ideas. Why don't I just say them when I'm with others?" The subpersonalities in her that could lead her to take risks, to be confident, and to assume leadership were not developed. "I'd love to be relaxed and easy going more of the time. It's fine when I am, but that's so seldom and it's only with Dan. Why aren't I that way for myself?" She was genuinely puzzled.

"What would you need to have happen to be more relaxed and easy going?" I asked her.

Immediately, she heard inside her head, "For your mother to die." I knew that wasn't a statement of physical fact – she wasn't talking about her biological mother – so I wanted to find the Mother part of Kate who was oppressing her.

In her imagery that day we were taken to another world peopled with figures in bright clothing. Kate reported her imagery to me:

> My mother and my second son are walking toward me. They're about a block's distance away but I can tell that they are each carrying something heavy. Just watching them I'm getting tense because I know they want to give me their burdens and I don't want to carry them. The muscles in my stomach and my shoulders are tight. How can I get away? My feet are in concrete boots buried in the earth so I can't walk . . . I need a shield to

protect me from them but I only have my tense muscles. They are closer now and I can't move. I can't get away and I can't stop them.

Then her imagery shifted suddenly. Kate saw herself in a steaming cauldron being stirred by a huge paddle. Holding the paddle was a Witch in a black robe (just as the Judge was always in a black robe). I asked if she could raise herself directly out of the cauldron, turn her back on the Witch, and float away. Kate said that when she raised herself out of the cauldron, she saw someone else in there with the Witch continuing to stir. She wasn't willing to leave the scene with anyone in the cauldron.

By now Kate was in tears. She was confronting her possible alternatives – to continue in her role as the recipient of the Witch/ Judge's oppressive whims or to cut her ties to that relationship altogether. She wanted to rescue the figure in the cauldron but she didn't know how and she was afraid of the Witch. She couldn't make the scene "turn out right."

Kate wrote in her journal at this time:

I can't force any changes on the Judge/Witch and I can't will her to disappear. She's a part of me and will always be with me in some form. I need to form a relationship with her. (The thought of asking her to talk to me is scary, but the less I know about her, about what she is feeling and thinking, the more impact she has on me. She can really beat me up if I ignore her. That scares me more!)

Kate then worked with the figures she had seen in the imagery session:

I needed a subpersonality who wasn't afraid of the Witch/Judge to form a relationship with her. So I called on Mark Twain. He asked the Judge to tell us about her childhood. (That seemed less scary.) She showed me an image of a pretty six-year-old girl with blond curls in a pink ribbon. The girl was standing with her toes behind a line that was painted on the floor. The little girl wanted very much to step over the line but feared the severe punishment which she knew would follow. The girl decided to be good, not to cross the line. She decided to become a proponent of those rules which restricted her instead of being the one restricted. (This kid wasn't going to be a Victim!) She became 'steely' inside so that she wouldn't feel her own disappointment about not venturing beyond her limits. She grew up as the Judge, relating to the world in a legalistic manner, not allowing gentleness or softness in her. The Judge had no close relationships and no one with whom she could share her conflicting feelings.

In our next session Kate asked Mark Twain to take the Judge back to the time in her childhood when the girl made the decision to deny her wants and be obedient to an external authority. At that point we played an alternative "tape." Kate viewed the scene in which the girl wanted to step across the line. I suggested, "This time the scene will develop differently. Put no effort into it, just watch and see what happens." Spontaneously, Kate saw a much larger figure place its hand on the girl's shoulders, letting the girl know that the action of stepping across the line would be acceptable. The girl proceeded and explored beyond the line, knowing that she was protected. The girl walked with comfort and confidence.

Kate followed the growth of that girl into adulthood and old age in her imagery. This time the figure developed into an Earth Mother rather than a Judge. Kate described her as a buxom, older woman dressed in a loose green and gold caftan. Her skin was dark and worn and her expression was gentle. The Earth Mother stated that her power would be used for enrichment not control.

Kate cried quietly for a few minutes. She had truly felt the shift in her Judge's rigidity which contained unhealed hurts and disappointments. There had been an opening, a letting go of fears, and a rush of aliveness. Intuitively, Kate understood immediately that the Judge had been using her "strength" to protect Kate from feeling her own hurt as Kate had at one time asked her to do. The Judge's rule orientation and stern manner hid Kate's childhood longing for love. When Kate saw this she felt a softening inside herself. The Judge's healing was manifest in the emergence of the Earth Mother.

This new figure symbolized healing but also facilitated healing. The Judge had experienced a transformation but the Dutiful Daughter still needed to move through her own healing. She didn't automatically heal as a result of the Judge's change. She still had the fear and longing which were rooted in the past.

The Earth Mother acknowledged the Dutiful Daughter's fear and saw her hidden anger. Because the Earth Mother could accept that the Dutiful Daughter was wounded and in pain behind her apparent compliance, she could help her to heal. The Earth Mother told the Dutiful Daughter to write about her resentments over the years toward the Judge. Kate allowed her Dutiful Daughter subpersonality to dominate and recorded her thoughts in her journal:

> I resent that you, Judge, have made me detach from my feelings of loneliness, anger, helplessness; that you never cared about me enough to talk with me or to listen to me; that you only wanted to shout orders at me; that you only gave me rules, not any part of yourself; that you were always busy "doing" a project and that you never had time just to be with me; that you laughed at my feelings or criticized them; that you were cruel to me when I needed you to help me; that everything was pretense for somebody else's benefit, nothing was sincere; that you were so controlling; and that you never apologized to me for hurting me.

Then the Earth Mother told the Dutiful Daughter to imagine that she spoke these words to the Judge and that the latter figure acknowledged them. In her imagery Kate heard the Judge from her past reply, "Yes, I understand what you're saying, but I am the way I am." Then the Dutiful Daughter truly saw the Judge as a person separate from herself. And when she understood that this former authority figure was the way she was because that was just her way and not because she, the Dutiful Daughter, was inadequate, she sighed and released her. Their old game of Control/Compliance was no longer interesting or necessary. The Dutiful Daughter didn't hope she could win. She saw the Judge from her past objectively and realized that she could respond by not reacting.

Over the next weeks Kate wrote:

As I watched the Dutiful Daughter detach from the Judge, I felt a release of her anger and depression. There was nothing left to resist or to please, there was no game and no hope of winning or fear of losing. The Dutiful Daughter felt acceptance and support from the Earth Mother without having to perform to receive it. She was confirmed. Now when I sense her presence, I can't call her the Dutiful Daughter. Her "duty" sprang from fear and that's not her motivation anymore.

She seems older, wiser, and calmer. Through her I had tried very hard, usually to my detriment, to gain from the Judge what the Earth Mother lovingly and freely gave. And now there seems to be an integration. The Earth Mother and the Dutiful Daughter have blended in a comfortable way. I feel more at home inside myself, less like I'm searching for something, not restless any more. I'm listening and responding to my feelings on an hourly basis. Oh, yes, and last night I dreamt that my mother had died and that I placed flowers on her grave. I loved her but she was gone.

It's not so much what happened to us a long time ago that creates the discomfort in our lives; it's how we maintain that same frustration and conflict within ourselves each day through our imbalanced subpersonality relationships. We are responsible for healing our subpersonalities. Controlling is never healing. **Just like people, subpersonalities grow and develop with attention and nurturing.** With the Earth Mother's acceptance and gentleness, Kate could realign her energy. When the original wound is acknowledged and felt, it will heal naturally and creatively.

Kate's inner selves had been interacting for years in ways that perpetuated the pain and frustration. It was her challenge to confront her inner imbalance and to correct it. By acknowledging that she was responsible for continuing her own woundedness through the dysfunctional interactions among her subpersonalities, Kate also implicitly acknowledged her responsibility for healing those interactions. If she could maintain imbalance, she could maintain balance.

Kate accepted her responsibility to integrate all her subpersonalities into her life by listening to them. The attempt to deal with feelings by denying them was abandoned in favor of maintaining communication among her subpersonalities. By keeping communication open, unexpected resolutions emerged.

Kate experienced a vitality she hadn't felt before. No longer did she know what she would do in every situation. Now she could be surprised and delighted by the unfolding guidance presented to her from within. As her subpersonalities lived peacefully together and felt nurtured in their needs, Kate sensed a growing aliveness and creativity in herself. Living her life with the participation of all her subpersonalities proved to be an adventure. She no longer responded out of fear but out of the joy and spontaneity which is natural for healthy subpersonalities. Her relationships with her husband and sons reflected her inner ease. They shared a deeper intimacy based on respect for each person's uniqueness and inner direction.

Are you thinking, "Well, that's fine and good for Kate, but I don't see people who aren't there and I definitely don't hear voices." Come on now. Don't you know exactly what your mother would say about that agreement you made last week? And about the way you talked to your friend? And about that encounter which left you so uncomfortable? You know your mother so well that she doesn't even have to be around for you to know what she would say. There is a part of you that is like a little Mother, whispering (or yelling) at you telling you to "Be sweet" or "Don't talk back" or whatever was your mother's favorite expression. There's a voice inside your head that says that to you all the time.

And there are other voices and other subpersonalities pulling and pushing you, too.

EXERCISE

Now you can do the same thing Kate did to contact her inner world figures. First, do the relaxation exercise on page 9. (Or, if you already have your own way of relaxing, do that now.) Then do the following exercise. (Again, it helps to record these instructions so that you may listen to them passively with your eyes closed.)

Allow an image to come to you of you walking. Just wait receptively until it comes in whatever way that is – in an picture, a memory, a feeling, or an impression. (Pause for thirty seconds) Where are you? Look all around you. Notice the details of your surroundings. (Pause) Are you inside or outside? (Pause) Now imagine the scene as though you were a bird and you were looking down on it. Which of your subpersonalities do you see? (Pause) If you are not sure of the name or label for the subpersonality, ask him/her. What do you hear? (Pause) Notice how that part of you moves. Does s/he walk smoothly and easily? (Pause) Is s/he carrying something? (Pause) Just from seeing the body posture, how would you guess the figure feels? (Pause)

Keep following this figure as s/he walks. S/he comes to a break in the walkway, perhaps a stream if s/he is outside or a wall if inside. What does the figure do? Just watch and notice what happens next. (Pause for three minutes)

Write about your imagery experience.

You may have noticed that while you were doing the exercise, you could stop thinking and watch the scene unfold. Could you allow yourself to be passive? Or was it a struggle for you not to be in charge of the action?

What was the obstacle and what happened there?

How is this characteristic of what happens in your life at blocked points?

Which subpersonalities react when you're frustrated? How does each of them react?

What part of you tells you how you should be? Allow yourself to relax, breathe deeply, and wait. An image of that figure that gives you your "shoulds" will come to you. Wait receptively until you see that figure. (Pause) What do you notice about that figure's appearance and demeanor?

Just by being in front of you, without using words, what message is that figure communicating?

What reaction do you notice in your body as it receives that message? What do you feel?

Let whatever is there be there inside you and keep breathing. Write any more feelings or associations you have to this exercise.

REFLECTIONS

What was your mother's (and now your internal Mother's) most frequent message to you?

And your father? Maybe he didn't put his wishes into words (or maybe he did), but you received messages from him about how he wanted you to be. What was his most frequent verbal or non-verbal message?

Just by watching how your father acted, you learned something about how to be. What did you learn?

By watching your mother what did you learn about how to be?

The development of your own internal Mother and Father took that learning inside you and made it part of who you are today. The significant people from your early life influenced the formation of your subpersonalities. You don't need to blame anyone from your past. Your Parent or Judge or Witch subpersonality is alive now and s/he's all yours! You received your cues from what you thought you saw with your real mother many years ago but now your internalized Mother calls the shots. She speaks to you a hundred times a day. You are always in relationship with her.

How do you relate to that Mother in you? Are you resisting her, resentful, adoring, appreciative but distant?

What do you fear about her?

What do you resent about the way she tries to control you?

What does your internalized Mother say to you (probably very subtly) which influences your behavior?

What do you like about her strength?

When you are strong what part of your strength comes from her?

In which of your behaviors do you notice your Father subpersonality? How would you describe your Father subpersonality?

What is his outstanding characteristic? What do you fear about him?

What do you resent about his attempts at control?

What does your internalized Father subpersonality say to you which influences your behavior?

What do you like about his strength?

When you are strong what part of your strength comes from him?

How much of your time and energy does your Father subpersonality receive?

How do your Mother and Father subpersonalities relate to each other inside you?

How and when do they conflict? How and when do they cooperate? Which subpersonality has the louder voice?

Who influences your choices about work? About friendship?

Chapter 4

OUR LIVES ARE PROJECTIONS

The patterns in our significant relationships reflect the way we treat ourselves. It's not possible to construct an outer reality which does not mirror the inner reality. They are two landscapes, one visible and one invisible, but they are exactly the same. Often we have masked the inner landscape with illusions, hopes, and fears so that it is hard for us to see it clearly, but the projection of our inner world onto the outer world never lies.

Projection involves seeing outside of you a reflection of what exists inside you. If I meet a woman whose husband continually abuses her and she chooses to stay with him, I know that some subpersonality inside of her doesn't nurture her feelings and needs. He acts out what exists within her. On an unconscious level, one of her subpersonalities believes another deserves abuse. She projects the abusive subpersonality while identifying with and acting out the abused Victim.

It really isn't possible to feel unworthy and to have others treat you as being worthy and valuable. Usually you will find another who will treat you exactly the way you (unconsciously) believe you deserve to be treated. It would be nice, wouldn't it, if our experience with others would offer some respite from the constant tearing down within our heads which we do to ourselves. But it seldom happens.

The unconscious is responsible for creating these projections in the outer world. We certainly wouldn't will some of the things which happen to us, but for anything that occurs, we need to consider: how have I contributed to creating this situation? It's like having an unseen light illuminate the shadowy recesses within us and then project them onto a movie set (our lives) for us to walk through. What we see around us is already operating within us. But it's so much easier to view when it's acted out around us by our family, friends, colleagues, acquaintances, or even the unwitting stranger who happens to cross our path. They don't know they're following our script, but they treat us exactly the way some subpersonality inside treats us. They're just easier to see. (And we're doing the same thing for them. We mirror some subpersonality and they react to us the way they react to that part of themselves.)

Our unconscious subpersonalities may want very different experiences for us from what we consciously say we prefer. We may say that we want to be wealthy but year after year we barely make ends meet. We may say that we want to be loved, but when a potential lover appears we shy away. We may say that we want to be fun-loving and popular, but we are restrained. What we say we want and how we act may be contradictory. By looking around us at what currently exists, we know what (unconsciously) we have chosen.

Why would our subpersonalities prefer pain or deprivation rather than love and abundance? Because we act according to feelings and beliefs which are not conscious. We cling to "truths" about ourselves which our rational Adult minds did not choose, but which have been manufactured by our Child minds in their attempts to make sense of reality. We think: Why would Dad hit me when he sees my toys on the floor? Because he loves me and wants me to learn responsibility. It's for my own good. He knows what's best for me. When I get hit, he's just telling me he loves me and wants the best for me. Or: Mom never has time for me. I guess I'm not an interesting person. Probably no one else will want to stay around me for long, either. After all if my own Mom can't love me how can I expect anyone else to love me? Or: Dad wasn't there for me when I needed protection. I guess I can't count on males. Or: Mom says she wants the best for me but she hates it when I cry. Crying must be a bad thing. I'll do what she likes and forget about what I feel.

By the time we're seven, our unconscious subpersonalities have contsructed an inner world based on our experience in the outer world when we were very young. We have internalized the world we lived in as children, in the form of different subpersonalities (an Abusive Man, a Submissive Woman, an angry but withdrawn Child, or whatever we experienced in our early lives). The outer world in which we first developed our childhood beliefs is now replicated in our heads. We have made an inner world in which our Child beliefs are confirmed and the old familiar patterns of relating are replicated.

We have created a complex world in our heads constructed out of old beliefs and we project this inner world onto our outer world. It may be hard to see our inner world but we can always see our outer world. We need to move through that world, not escape it. We can't tunnel under it or fly over it. It exists. Our beliefs (which we probably don't know we hold) form our realities. What we see around us reflects what we (unconsciously) believe to be true. The form in which our beliefs are manifest can help us to discover what the beliefs are. The form itself isn't important. What creates the form – our unconscious beliefs – is. And these beliefs "live" in our subpersonalities.

Only dating ungiving men tells you that one of your subpersonalities is ungiving. Perhaps the belief that your inner Male holds is that your Child doesn't deserve gentleness. Frequently meeting angry women tells you that you have an angry female subpersonality who is trying to be heard by you. Perhaps her belief is that she must wipe away neediness with anger in order to be safe.

When we see patterns in our encounters, we know a subpersonality is active, wanting to communicate with us. When we can't hear from our subpersonalities directly, they will use another person's voice to get our attention. If you have a strong reaction to someone, positive or negative, you are probably seeing and hearing one of your own subpersonalities reflected; that's what the intensity of your reaction is about.

When we feel blocked in reaching our goals – professional, financial, or relational – we need to look to the inner world. Our subpersonalities are in conflict. The way we learned to handle conflicts as children will be re-created among our subpersonalities. Perhaps in your home when you were growing up a controlling parent didn't listen to your feelings (Child). Today your inner Parent figure may try to dominate your Scared Child.

After many years of practicing a certain imbalanced pattern of interacting – Controlling Parent/Submissive Child, Angry Critic/Rebellious Teenager, Ascetic Monk/Frivolous Flirt, or whatever our primary subpersonality conflict is – we find ourselves stuck. Without our realizing it, the rules have changed. No longer is the world responding to us as it did when we were living out of balance. We can't be successful in the imbalanced ways we were successful previously and suddenly there isn't anything we can do to make life turn out as we want. Then we need to go inside, for the outer reflection won't change until the inner landscape does. Always the first step in change is to acknowledge *what is*.

Whatever we choose (and we can see what we've chosen by looking around us), for some reason seems the best compromise. Often it appears to be safe. We may want spontaneity, freedom, and appreciation, but feeling safe comes first. So, the subpersonalities have reached an acceptable equilibrium in *what is*. There is something good about the way things are right now and we need to discover what that is.

If we don't like what we see around us, a natural inclination is to try to change what we see that we don't like. But, as we realize that our outer reality is simply a reflection of an inner belief system, we will find it much faster and easier to change what within us is blocking us. **The outer world won't change until the inner world has changed**. It's no use trying to change a mirror if you don't like the reflection.

Perhaps our inner Ambitious Entrepreneur wants to be a millionaire but the Deprived Child believes that having anything for herself is dangerous. Or the Lover may want to be married but the Rejected Child believes that no one will stay with her. Or the Successful Professional can only function when the Loser is out of sight. We have been able to achieve some of what the Entrpreneur or the Lover or the Professional wants by ignoring and pushing away the secondary subpersonality. But the time always comes when that imbalance resulting from the alienation of some subpersonality is no longer tolerable to the unconscious. The frustration one subpersonality experiences in attempting to reach her goals spotlights the opposite needs/beliefs of another subpersonality. And now we have to acknowledge those needs (and that less acceptable subpersonality) which we have thus far ignored.

Some people refuse to recognize that they have any responsiblity for creating their reality. Victims don't acknowledge the concurrence of their outer world with their inner. Victims prefer to accept no responsibility for creating their lives and give all the responsibility (and blame) to others. They maintain an inner imbalance and identify with one subpersonality (the Helpless Child) and ignore and, therefore, project another subpersonality (a Tyrant). They see it only in someone else, not in themselves.

I always feel victimized by Victims. They place total responsiblity for their feelings onto me without recognizing the strong pull they emit. They, unconsciously, need someone to mistreat them. They need me to be their Bad Guy so that they may continue their Victim denial.

Relating to Victims is frustrating. I sense a pull from their unconscious asking me to mistreat them and I refuse but have to struggle with the tension within me. If they are subtle and practiced at being a Victim, I am sucked into their game unawares and end up saying something which shocks me with its callousness. Then their view of the world as cruel and ungiving has been confirmed again through me.

In fact, those of us who come into contact with Victims are very responsive to them. They just won't see that we do exactly what they, unconsciously, ask us to do. They need to remain Victims to continue their denial and avoidance of responsibility. If they truly took responsibility, they would have to consider their part in contributing to a reality in which they are always the Helpless Child and someone else always has the power. They don't give their own internal Responsible Adult time or energy. They refuse to see the restrictive controlling Tyrant subpersonality inside of themselves, but they see it everywhere outside.

We all, to some extent, "get" people to react to us in response to our dominant subpersonality. It's unconscious on our parts and on theirs. We end up in a dance to an unheard tune. We collude with them and they with us. Every Victim, therefore, needs to engage a Victimizer in his/her dance. How else can s/he play the Victim?

* * * *

When she was young, Sharon's parents were emotionally cold, neglectful, and abusive. She felt rejected. Actually she probably was rejected. Her parents didn't want a child and didn't want to hear her Child feelings and needs. Sharon left home after her emotionally tumultuous junior high and high school years and hasn't spoken with her parents for over twenty years.

Short and slender, Sharon is an attractive woman in her early forties, with narrow wide set dark eyes, and curly ash brown hair. A characteristic mannerism for Sharon is clenching her fists and slightly squinting her eyes. She punctuates her sentences with these gestures for emphasis. She crosses her legs and an unseen motor drives her foot rhythmically in the air. Her small body seems tightly coiled, tension compressed in all her muscles.

On every special occasion – her birthday, Christmas, Mother's Day – Sharon is disappointed. She doesn't believe that her husband and her two children love her enough or give her enough attention. Regardless of what her family does, she ends the day in tears, feeling rejected. This pattern has continued for years. Her children feel frustrated by their inability to convince her of their caring and her husband refuses to try to assuage her unloved feelings any longer.

The years of disappointments were draining, however, and finally exhausted, Sharon was unwilling to repeat the cycle of hope, disappointment, frustration, and depression that her Child played out. She didn't want to live this way any longer but didn't know how to pull herself out of this self-destructive pattern. So she decided to try therapy. During our second session, I suggested that some other subpersonality was needed to intervene. Sharon agreed and we started our imagery work.

With her eyes closed Sharon invited the part of her with strong feelings to show itself. She received an image of her Rejected Child as a fat, ten-year-old girl. Her hair was braided and she wore plaid shorts. Either she walked in a small circle or sat in a corner with her head down. She was the picture of despair.

When she spoke, the Child sounded fearful and pathetic. She whined, "No one cares, no one ever has, no one could possibly love me. Something's wrong with me. I'm not like other people. I don't know why not. Something's missing in me. Even when people act like they love me, pretty soon they don't love me anymore. No one stays around." And she cried.

This Child was convinced of the hopelessness of ever receiving the love she wanted because of some unnamed deficiency on her part. When she watched the Rejected Child, Sharon again felt the pain she knew so well, embodied in the Child. And, just like the Child, Sharon didn't know what to do.

Sharon truly was a pathetic figure when she was identified with the Rejected Child. Her shoulders drooped, she sighed and her voice became faint. I could understand why someone would want to rescue her from this misery.

I could also understand why that someone would leave her. Sharon was completely identified with her miserable Rejected Child! When she was overwhelmed with the Child's needs and hopelessness, no other voice could be heard. She couldn't even see that anyone else existed. She was as blind to real people outside of her as she was to other subpersonalities inside of her. The Rejected Child believed that no one could love her and she wasn't really open to any contrary evidence.

In the end, the Rejected Child always proved herself right.

She spotted the rejection she expected. No matter how long it took or how much reinterpretation of events she had to do, her belief that no one would love her (in the way she wanted) was eventually confirmed. Maintaining that belief seemed ultimately important. "Of course," she would utter, "I only get left behind. Nobody really loves me. Other people love and are loved back. But, me? No, it doesn't happen for me. I don't know why but what is freely given to everyone else is denied to me." And this time there was an angry edge to her tears.

I knew that first we had to lessen Sharon's total identification with this Child. I wanted her to be aware of the Child but to *look* at her, not to *be* her. I also wanted her to open to the other figures inside her. She couldn't imagine that any other part existed.

Assuming the stance of Observer of the Rejected Child released Sharon's identication with her. She practiced inviting the Child to speak and watched her as though she were sitting in a movie theatre and the Child were on the screeen. By staying in her Observer no matter what the Child was saying, Sharon learned to identify with the Observer part of herself and not to react. The Observer didn't judge or try to change what she observed. She only watched.

After Sharon (Observer) listened to her Rejected Child, she thanked the Child for expressing herself verbally and let her go. As long as Sharon could hear the Child's words, she didn't have to act out the Child's drama. The Observer noticed that the Child usually maintained a low level depression but that some-times she became overwhelmed with hopelessness. Sharon recorded this blip in the Child's pattern in her mental notebook and continued watching the girl. She checked in with her every few days and just noticed how the Child was feeling and what she was doing. (When you check in with these inner world figures they are often going about their lives, thinking the way they think, doing what they do. It's like peeking into someone's window.)

Sharon, in her Observer, often saw the Child playing by herself, usually indoors with her head down. She didn't seem to get any exercise or talk to anyone else or to go outside. "She's making life hard for herelf," was Sharon's comment after seeing her Child in this self contained world so many times. "I wouldn't let my own children act like that. I'd push them out the door, at least. This kid is waiting for someone to rescue her!"

This Rejected Child was a challenge for Sharon to watch and not try to change but Sharon talked with her every few days over the next weeks. Always she heard the same message:

"No one loves me. No one sticks around."

During one period of the hopelessness that intermittently overtook the girl, Sharon invited any other subpersonality to speak to her. Her Observer guessed that someone else must be active because the Child's usual low level depression, which the Observer had come to know, wasn't normally puctuated by this acute hopelessness. Something unnoticed was happening.

It took awhile but over several days in which the Observer was present and waited, another figure began to differentiate herself. An image of an older woman became clear. "Severe" described her tighty pulled back hair, her fitted clothing, and her drawn facial expression. Her air was self righteous as she looked down her long pointed nose. She felt virtuous knowing that the Rejected Child was suffering. Her job seemed to be to continue the Child's pain. When Sharon realized this, she called the new figure the Victimizer.

"I can't believe this Victimizer lives inside me! I have never thought of myself as a mean person but this Victimizer intends harm." And Sharon's inner world took on the full dimensions of her life. Now she owned the Victimizer as hers. "I can't say I like knowing that I'm a Victimizer but if she's really there (and now I can't deny that she is) well, then, I have to admit it."

As she learned to discriminate more and more finely what was going on behind the Child's helplessness, Sharon heard the Victimizer's words. This figure told the Rejected Child that other people were responsible for her suffering. "They betrayed you. You don't have to tolerate that." The Victimizer did not take responsibility for her own part in the Child's pain. She said, "I need the Rejected Child to suffer. She has suffered for so long and she knows how it will end (she always acts surprised but really she's not). It's comfortable. Always predictable. We have a system that's working just fine."

The Victimizer fueled the Child's suffering and wanted it to continue. She gave the Child messages which deflated her. The Child didn't evaluate the messages, she just swallowed them whole and felt the resultant depressed feelings. The Victimizer worked to keep the Child in pain. Sharon watched the Victimizer for several weeks. She wanted to know her and to understand how she thought. So she would question her during our imagery sessions. One time she asked the Vicimizer if she didn't want to be happy and heard, "I am doing fine." With that Sharon understood that this Victimizer wanted to maintain the status quo. She was satisfied with things just the way they were.

"Why is this Victimizer so angry?" Sharon wondered. "She's beating up on a helpless Child, she knows the Child is suffering, and yet this Victimizer wants no changes. What gives?"

In her real (outer world) life Sharon didn't allow herself to be angry. She was quiet, usually non-responsive, in fact, she was often overlooked. "Am I invisible?" she questioned. To many people she was. She didn't want her anger to be seen and if that entailed hiding all of her she would do it.

What are we to do if we judge a natural part of ourselves "unacceptable"? Usually, we (without awareness) push it into our Shadows so we're not aware of it. We think we have made it disappear but we've just tucked it out of sight. And there it lives underground – gathering power and doing whatever it wants unchecked. That's where Sharon's anger was – in her unconscious Shadow, unseen and unsupervised in the form of the Victimizer.

Since Sharon was introverted (she directed her energy inside her), the Victimizer directed her anger towards Sharon's Child. She wouldn't direct it toward her parents, the apparent withholding source of love. By siding with the now long gone parents, the Victimizer punished the Child for not being what her parents wanted. And so, the Child was rejected by the Victimizer inside Sharon just as she had been rejected by her parents many years before!

The Child received the Victimizer's anger and believed it fit her. She honestly believed what she told Sharon, "There's something missing in me. I'm not OK." The Observer noticed that the Child thought that being depressed was being good – doing just what an older subpersonality (the Victimizer) wanted. The Child was willing to do anything which made her OK. At least the Child was getting approval from someone, even if she had to hurt to get it.

When the Child began to feel better or to hope that her experience would be more joyful, then the Victimizer began with her messages again. She repeatedly told the Child that she was unlovable. These messages were so subtle that Sharon's Child had been hearing them for years without questioning them. It didn't even seem like a distinct voice; to the Child it was just the truth.

Thus, in her quest for love, the Child had a need to suffer – that was how she would receive the Victimizer's "love". She was being good when she was depressed. Her life was predictable and no one could surprise her – she wasn't going to be so vulnerable as to receive love that might be snatched away.

As the Victimizer's malevolent intent became clearer, another subpersonality spontaneously arose. A masculine figure in his forties said,

I don't like what I see happening between the Victimizer and the Rejected Child. The Victimizer is abusing the Child, who doesn't know how to take care of herself. The Child can't put limits on the Victimizer. The Child needs protection.

Sharon named this new subpersonality the Reasonable Adult. In his three piece business suit with a hanging watch band, this Adult was outraged by the behavior of the Victimizer and wanted to intervene.

Sharon watched these figures interact. She noticed how the Child took center stage, with the Victimizer always close but unseen in the shadows. When the Child felt hopeless Sharon listened for the voice of the Victimizer. And she always found it. The Child felt very sad when the Victimizer said: "You're unlovable. No one will ever stay with you." Two sides of the same coin – the Child's pain and the Victimizer's words. Sharon learned that when one was present so was the other.

The Child totally believed the Victimizer and was not sophisticated enough to confront her. But when Sharon could identify clearly what her Rejected Child felt and what her Victimizer said, she could call on her Reasonable Adult. He wanted the Child to be free of the Victimizer's oppressive statements. To the Victimizer he said, "Your words are not the truth. You hate and hurt. You don't want joy and happiness. You are committed to suffering and separation between the Child and anyone else."

The Reasonable Adult could see that the Victimizer was trying to protect the Child from even greater hurt by keeping her in a state of lesser but continuous pain. This "lesser" pain kept the Child afraid of closeness, so that she would never risk the greater pain that can ensue from loving in a truly open hearted way. The Victimizer offered the Child manufactured pain instead of being vulnerable to the real pain that may happen in an undefended life.

The Reasonable Adult didn't agree to the bargain to stay safe and less alive by staying depressed. And he was vehement in his protest. "We will take whatever life naturally brings our way. We will not" (and he emphasied NOT in a louder voice) "be organized into a neat structure of constant longing to avoid the real hurt of the real rejection from the past. We have every right to feel that!!!"

By clearly describing the dynamics between the Child and the Victimizer, he educated the Child and helped her see. In this way, the Victimizer was brought out of the shadows.

But then the Child's voice became audible. She said, "I really do want someone to love me." Now Sharon knew to look inside her, not outside. Sharon guessed that there must be a subpersonality who could be a good parent to the Child.

Sharon asked to be shown an image of that inner figure. She closed her eyes, breathed, and waited. Watching her spontaneous imagery, Sharon described a Mother. "She is dressed in a long, full-skirted calico dress. She resembles a pioneer woman. She looks like she established a home in the wilderness."

I suggested to Sharon that she invite the Pioneer Mother to establish a home inside of Sharon for her Child. Sharon (the Observer) did so and watched. She saw the Pioneer Mother clean a small cabin, bringing in flowers and fixing a meal of fresh vegetables. The Mother arranged a corner where she could hold the Child and tell her stories.

Sharon was surprised by the industriousness of this figure as she prepared a space in which to care for the Child. The Pioneer Mother readied herself to welcome the Child by spending a few minutes alone with her eyes closed. Then she looked up and called to the Child who came slowly from around a corner. The Pioneer Mother invited her to sit on her lap. The Child crawled up hesitantly and waited to see what would happen to her. The Pioneer Mother sang softly and rocked the Child.

After several minutes, the Child's body relaxed and she rested her head on the Mother's breast. The Mother continued to sing and hum and the Child dozed. Even while the Child slept, the Mother held her and sang so that when the Child awoke she was still being rocked.

With variations, this scene occurred weekly. The Child became accustomed to the constancy of the Mother's reassuring presence. She grew into a "body understanding" of what receiving care and attention felt like. Usually the Child would sleep and her body would soak up the caring from the Pioneer Mother's enfolding larger body. The transfer of love was unconscious between the Mother and the Child as Sharon watched.

Sharon saw the Child grow taller and slimmer, feeling confident and strong. The Child incorporated the Mother's concern for her and she grew up having concern for herself. Her body knew she had a home even when she didn't focus her thoughts upon that fact.

As Sharon watched these scenes of the Pioneer Mother and the Child, her own real life adult experience shifted. She wrote in her journal:

Within myself I am comfortable and with others I am happy. My inner Child has received the caring she so desperately wanted and now other people seem supportive and loving to me! When I saw the reactions of my husband and children change, I had to realize that in the past I had been instrumental, without even knowing it, in affecting how they treated me. Now that

I'm listening more to the Mother within me, I receive more love from around me.

Now that I experience my life working the way I want it to, I realize that I haven't been depressed and oppressed all of these years because my real parents rejected me. All I was doing by blaming my parents was refusing to take responsibility for my own life, for how that inner Victimizer was oppressing and rejecting my Child every day. When I saw how dramatically my experience shifted after the internal work I did, without my parents' involvement, I fully understood that my parents were not responsible for my pain today, but that my Victimizer was.

There was a time in Sharon's childhood when she wasn't responsible for the experiences of her life. Children cannot be blamed for any miserable situations in which they live. But the role Sharon had learned during childhood (Rejected Child) was continued during adulthood without regard to her situation in reality. **Just as children cannot be blamed for their suffering, adults cannot blame their suffering on anyone else**.

Sharon's process shows how she needed to hold onto her old beliefs, act them out in relationships, experience the loneliness, and finally realize how she was responsible for maintaining her pain through her Victimizer. She wrote in her journal:

I realize now that we're all in this life together. No one gets a head start. We can walk with each other or push everyone away but we're all walking the same path. It's more important to learn how to walk the path than to resent the other walkers. Walking with integrity and responsibility is the real challenge.

* * * *

We interact with others in the same way that our subpersonalities are interacting among themselves. We project one of our subpersonalities onto someone in our lives and then totally identify with another subpersonality. Many of us believe that we shouldn't be powerful personally, that is, we shouldn't accept our own needs and wants and guidance. We believe it is better to keep others comfortable and to maintain silence. Since we aren't comfortable owming our power, we project it. When we project power onto husbands, wives, or friends, we remove them from the realm of being peers and structure a Parent-Child relationship. It seems that we need to continually create unequal power situations in which we can experience our feelings about being powerless until we can change them into experiences in which we are powerful. This process takes many repetitions.

We gradually become aware that we can have some control over how we are treated. We can't just let go of an image of ourselves as deprived and mistreated and, overnight, assume the position of an effective, respectable soul. There is no going directly from the Frog to the Prince. The steps are small and the transformation gradual, but it does occur.

Alice's husband seemed very powerful to her. Most adults seemed very powerful to Alice. She felt small, insignificant, and unworthy of notice, just as she had as a child. Then, her mother had dominated her three daughters and her husband, not considering their wants or feelings, not even acknowledging them as having lives separate from her. When her mother wanted to go somewhere, everyone went. When she wanted to stay, no one's alternative suggestion was allowed. Her mother's wishes always prevailed.

Alice had learned from watching her father that the way to get what she wanted was to be invisible and passive-aggressive, to indirectly and non-verbally assert herself. Her father had lived this way with his controlling wife without losing his own individuality. He had subtly and quietly resisted her. When she wanted to go, he would get ready, but at the last minute he couldn't find something he needed, so the family would wait. When she chose to stay, he was restless, grumbling and irritable, interfering with her peace. Without saying much, he made his presence uncomfortably felt.

Without realizing it, by living with her father Alice had learned how to affect others without taking responsibility for her actions. She had developed a "powerless" subpersonality who annoyed people. "Who me?" this subpersonality seemed to be saying. "I don't know what you're talking about. I'm not doing anything." And then Alice would do whatever this figure wanted regardless of the impact it had on others. Thus, Alice was quite effective in getting what she wanted without being responsible and adult about it. And she didn't even know she was doing it.

Alice's personal power scared her. She feared the consequences of stating her feelings and her wants clearly. Since she wanted very much to be taken care of, she wouldn't risk exposing any part of herself she thought others would dislike. She wanted to maintain connections to potential caregivers regardless of the cost. And the cost was her integrity.

She believed that expressing her natural impulses would lead to abandonment. In her mind it wasn't OK to say, "I want" or "I feel." Being "known" was dangerous. It was wrong to be an individual and to stand out. Therefore, her own wants and preferences took on an ominous quality. If she expressed them honestly and directly, she didn't know what reaction she might receive. But she was too afraid to find out.

She also didn't know the limits of her own unbridled aggression. She had felt her rage at times and it had terrified her. What will I do? she asked herself. How far will I go if I don't restrain myself? What irreparable damage will I cause? What will my family do if they truly see who I am?). Thus, she lost her spontaneity and her trust for her feelings.

A subpersonality developed who housed those parts of Alice she feared would lead her to ultimate aloneness. She called it the Little Devil. The Devil contained her strong feelings, her assertiveness, and her wants. Like Alice's father, the Devil was concerned with resisting the control of others. This resistance was the only way Alice knew to be "powerful."

Her husband said that Alice was very effective in gaining what she wanted. She nagged, cried, and complained. And always she felt resentful. She felt herself to be a Victim and she didn't understand how she could be otherwise. She wanted someone to take care of her, to understand her needs and wants without her having to verbalize them.

Alice's appearance betrayed the quality of care she took of herself. She was generally disordered, her wrinkled shirts and skirts almost, but not quite, matching. Her hair was seldom arranged neatly and often was not clean. She gave the impression that she had just rolled out of bed, barely able to keep our appointment. She seemed to have emerged from chaos with adequate respectability to appear in the office but not set to continue her day. There was always the sense of something left unfinished. I guessed that she didn't usually make her bed.

Her hazel eyes seldom met mine. Instead she examined her nails, the furniture, and the ceiling. She seemed not to want to relate to me too directly. I wondered if she really knew what I looked like.

Alice believed that her role in life should be to make others comfortable by anticipating their needs and providing what they wanted. (This was how she wanted others to treat her, too.) She cared for her family and didn't listen to her own wants or live her own life from any inner direction. She didn't recognize her belief that because she didn't take care of herself it was others' responsibility to do so. This unspoken deal didn't work for her – she didn't receive the attention she wanted and she wouldn't express her frustration directly. Her Devil was kept hidden, unconscious, but still very angry.

As her three children left home, her husband, Hank, tired of her whining and spent little time with her. Her passive-aggressive manipulations were futile; there was no one around who would react to her. Now she couldn't focus on anyone else. She recognized that her own life wasn't satisfying but she wanted other people to change to be more indulgent with her. She wasn't yet ready to acknowledge that *she* would have to be the one to change.

As is always the case, we go as far as we can using the strengths we naturally have until they prove inadequate. Then we have to work to develop additional resources. Since Alice had emphasized the feminine trait of nurturing through so much of her life, we looked for a masculine voice inside her which would provide balance. For several weeks she was quiet in her closed eye sessions, watching for signs of a masculine presence.

Eventually, she met a subpersonality she called John.

He was a middle-aged man who was submissive, gentle, and sweet. A pleasant but ineffectual figure, John looked like Alice's father. Alice liked John immediately and found talking to him comforting. John knew all the right things to say to Alice to make her feel appreciated. ("You've been so unselfish. You're a fine mother.") However, she felt John's lack of power. He was "nice" but she didn't think he was strong.

After several more weeks in which Alice listened quietly, she heard another masculine voice. Greg was rough, uncouth, and aggressive – unlike anyone Alice knew. She described him as a "drunken biker." Alice recoiled from approaching him directly. She didn't like or trust Greg. She found him "offensive" and was embarrassed that he was a part of her. She didn't want to talk to him or listen to him. She hoped he would just disappear.

One day, she was mugged by a man who stole her purse. Alice was terribly upset. In our session the next afternoon, she asked Greg if he knew anything about the incident. He replied, "Yes, I knew what was happening. I saw the entire scene. And I wanted it to happen to you. You ignore me, but a man finally got to you. Maybe now you've learned your lesson."

Greg had chosen this dramatic way to get her attention. When Alice heard him say that, she realized that this subpersonality could affect her physically as well as emotionally. She thought she was escaping him when she ignored him, but she only made him more destructive.

If Greg had known what had happened to her, he probably was also involved in creating it, Alice surmised. When she asked him if he were, he said, "Yes," but offered no explanation.

She was angry with Greg for his part in the mugging and now felt like his Victim. But she also realized that she needed to take him seriously. Ignoring him was costly emotionally and dangerous physically. She had preferred to pretend that he didn't exist but could no longer afford the consequences of that denial.

Alice spent time listening to Greg over the next weeks. She wasn't anxious to know him; she was just terrified of what might happen to her if she didn't. When she paid attention to him, he responded to her honestly and directly. She still didn't like him, but she respected him as she got to know him.

Alice asked him questions about how he thought and when he consistently emphasized the need to be assertive, she consulted him about business concerns. (She didn't trust him enough yet to talk about her feelings.) Greg advised her to negotiate in a forthright manner and to be assertive about what she wanted.

Because she was listening to him, he didn't hurt her surreptitiously. Greg encouraged Alice to identify with him and let him do the talking when she needed to make a business deal. He didn't care if anyone else liked him, he just wanted to get what he thought he deserved. During this time Alice was scheduled to negotiate a new contract at work. Previously, her Victim would have entered the meeting unprepared and left feeling unsatisfied and resentful. But this time Greg asked to be in charge and Alice agreed. He planned his short speech and outlined his requirements. Alice was totally professional and everything that Alice/Greg requested was included in her new contract.

Alice used Greg successfully in several more negotiations and was pleased with the results. There was no emotional wrangling and no guilt. In fact, emotions didn't come into the picture at all.

Even though she could appreciate what Greg offered her in business dealings, Alice was still angry with him for "participating" in the mugging. She told him so (having learned assertion from him) and then asked for an apology. Greg replied,

The mugging was something you forced to happen. You didn't listen to me and didn't even want to know I existed. The Selfless Caretaker was the only person you wanted to hear from. Well, it's too bad the mugging had to happen but you could have treated me differently.

When we push parts of ourselves out of our awareness and ignore them they gain power and intensity. They continue to operate but without our awareness. Consequently, we don't know what they are doing. They still exist, and because we no longer oversee their actions, they may behave destructively and we are blind to it. We have wanted to keep them in the dark but *we* are really in the dark because we have chosen to ignore that part of ourselves. That, essentially, allows the unwanted subpersonality total freedom without our monitoring awareness, which can be very dangerous. It is likely we will feel the result with intense pain. We can't ignore any part of ourselves and escape untouched. What we have chosen to keep unconscious, gets acted out towards, or within, the body. Choosing not to listen to the unconscious has serious physical consequences.

Alice felt forced to relate to Greg in self-defense. She didn't want his anger directed at her again. Although she didn't want to admit that any part of her had the characteristics she ascribed to Greg, she had to acknowledge that there was an irrefutable correlation between her denial of him and her feeling victimized by other people.

This became clear to her through her journal writing. It wasn't anyone in particular she could accuse of trying to hurt her; she was just the Loser in general. After acknowledging her subpersonalities and listening to them, Alice understood that she was making her life turn out as it was. Unconsciously, she had been clinging to her Victim/Loser identity and repressing Greg. Now, after so much pain, Alice thought that she was ready to relinquish the Loser subpersonality. In her journal, her Adult wrote:

I don't know how it has happened but losing has become my m.o. in relation to everyone and everything. I have the feeling that everyone wants to take something from me. I never think that anyone would want to talk to me or be interested in my opinions.

At that moment Greg intruded:

Greg: You don't want to know *my* opinions. You only talk to me because you're afraid of what will happen to you if you don't.

Adult: Are you saying that I treat you the way other people treat me?

Greg: I'm saying that you need to acknowledge how you mistreat me. You ignore me and stifle my voice and then you whine when you feel treated that way by others. Well, I say hooray! You're only getting what you deserve. You think you can just decide that I don't exist and "poof", I'll disappear. Well, damn it, you're going to acknowledge me somehow!

Adult: Whoa. You are very upset.

Greg: Damn right! So are you when you feel ignored. You should understand exactly how I feel!

Adult: I'm blocking you out and you're reacting the same way I do? I never realized what I was doing!

Greg: You've been so self-righteous! You make me sick with all your complaining about how much you give and how little support you receive and then you turn around and suffocate me! Well, I won't let you kill me, you bitch. I'm going to live as long as you do and every time you hurt me, you're going to get it right back! Don't think you're stronger than I am. You may win small victories, but I'll never let you be at peace as long as you judge me "offensive". Perhaps I am offensive, but what I'm offended at is your high and mighty attitude that you're so good and I'm so awful. Bullshit!! I'll show you awful!

Adult: OK, OK. I had no idea you were so upset. The way you explain it, your feelings are perfectly understandable. It's healthy that you don't want to die. And I've been trying to kill you! We've been warring and I didn't even know it! Let's not do this any longer. We can find another way to exist together. We don't need to fight constantly.

Greg: I only fight because you force me to. I will not be killed!

Adult: I will not kill you, I promise. I will offer you what I want – acceptance. I will listen to you and not judge you.

Greg didn't respond but my Adult sensed that he was no longer furious. I've opened a door for him. He doesn't need to bang on it.

Over the next months, Alice's Adult listened to Greg. Sometimes he ranted irrationally, sometimes he criticized her, and sometimes he just told her what he wanted. No matter what he said, Alice's Adult listened and accepted it.

As the Adult's attitude toward Greg shifted from one of disdain to one of acknowledgement, his manner changed also. Gradually, he became softer. He spoke more slowly and swore less. He seemed to feel more relaxed as the threat of annihilation by the Adult was removed.

Alice spent many hours talking with and observing Greg and John. She learned when the personal style of each of them was appropriate to her situation and she called on them as she needed to. In the next weeks, as Greg's "softening" continued, Alice could no longer distinguish him from John. Initially, they had such different personalities. But as Greg's hostility diminished so did

John's passivity. They seemed to be moving from opposite ends of a continuum toward a center point. This was not something Alice had thought about and chosen. She just watched this merging happen as she stayed open to each of them. This new masculine figure had the genuine caring of John and the appropriate assertiveness of Greg without either one's weakness – Greg's bulldozing aggression or John's passive-aggressive compliance. Alice finally grew to trust her new masculine figure. She committed herself to always listening to him. Alice knew that he welcomed her commitment because her interactions with others were gratifying. She took that as a reflection.

She wrote in her journal:

> I suppose the changes have been slow in coming. Over these last two years, my marriage has become totally different from how it was for ten years before that. Hank has begun courting me again! I had forgotten the little bouquets of wild flowers he used to bring me, but now they have reappeared.

And there are other nice touches that remind me of our affection. When we were polarized into our roles – my Child/his Parent, my Victim/his Jerk – we didn't trust each other. We didn't share vulnerability. We wouldn't get too close to each other but we couldn't let go, either. We just maintained a resentful stalemate.

Sometimes there were angry eruptions after which we didn't speak for two or three days, but mostly we believed (I can see now) that the other was the adversary, someone to be scrutinized and to be wary of. We never could fully relax around each other. Yet, when we tried parting, we feared losing the other's protection. I hated Hank for his lack of response to me, but the thought of not having his stabilizing influence in my life terrified me. I needed him, but feared him, and that usually showed in my little ways of pressuring him and putting him down.

Now I look for my own protection from inside me and not from Hank. It's hard work looking at what is happening inside me.

Being a Victim is easy. It's taking responsibility for my feelings and growing up that's hard. But that's the only way Hank and I can share true friendship – as equal, healthy partners.

Because Alice had worked to create and maintain an inner peace, her outer relationships were also peaceful. There was no internal warfare to be reflected in external circumstances, only cooperation, and caring inside her and around her. When she maintained peace within her, she experienced it around her.

Do you identify with Sharon or Alice? How?

Describe your own Victim subpersonality. Include descriptions of gender, appearance, age, behavior.

When are you identified with your Victim subpersonality? Can you recall an instance recently when your Victim was prominent?

What is the characteristic statement you make to yourself or to others when your Victim dominates?

When does it "work" to be a Victim? What is the payoff?

What's going on inside you when you choose to act out the Victim subpersonality?

Which other subpersonality in you could achieve what the Victim achieves but in a more direct, responsible way?

EXERCISE

Spend several minutes doing the Relaxation exercise on page 9 and then do the following imagery exercise.

See yourself walking on a city street. Notice what is on your left and your right. (Pause) There are people walking past you. Look at their faces. (Pause) Some of the people represent your subpersonalities. One of them will come up to you. Wait. (Pause) When a figure approaches you notice the body posture, and facial expression of the figure. (Pause) Listen as that figure speaks to you. S/he will tell you something about him/herself. (Pause) What part of you is s/he? (Pause) What is his/her message to you? (Pause) Thank him/her and walk on. (Pause)

Does another figure approach you? Wait and watch. (Pause) Notice who comes and what s/he says to you. (Pause) Again, thank him/her and let him/her pass. If all the figures so far have been of the same gender, see if there is anyone of the opposite gender who wants to approach you. (Pause) Walk for as long as you would like. Does another figure approach you? (Pause)

Now as you walk there are no other people around. Think about the messages you have been given. (Pause) Notice how you breathe and how you walk. (Pause)

REFLECTIONS

Describe each figure you met and the message from each figure. What happened inside your body as you heard each message?

How does your body manifest your beliefs and conflicts? Do you have chronic health concerns?

Do you get cravings? For what? Where do you hold your tension?

What could you be holding onto with that tension? What feelings are you avoiding?

Who is your seldom-heard-from inner masculine figure? Who is your seldom-heard-from inner feminine figure?

Of all the figures you saw during your walk, whom do you like and whom do you dislike?

Which of the subpersonalities you mentioned wants your attention? Take a few minutes, listen to that subpersonality, and record what you hear.

Chapter 5

DEVELOPING A CARING PARENT

Jane is a beautiful woman, tall and slender. Her subtle make-up emphasizes her large blue eyes. Her purse, shoes, and nails match her coordinated outfit. In contrast to her "together" appearance, she seems uncomfortable on her first visit with me, swinging her foot, speaking quickly, and seldom making eye contact. She later admits that she was embarrassed about needing a therapist.

The issue that brings Jane into therapy is her intense sadness and frustration over not conceiving a child. She has been to all kinds of doctors; had two minor surgeries; dragged her husband, Mike, to examinations; tried artificial insemination and donor sperm. She kept charts and calendars and took her temperature daily. She did everything she was instructed to do, but getting pregnant was not something she could force by her own determination. If it were a matter of following directions, Jane would have accomplished her goal. But becoming pregnant was not a problem she could solve by taking action.

Mike is a recovering alcoholic; he hasn't had a drink for eight years. Jane has supported the two of them for most of their thirteen year marriage. Regularly there are crises, usually financial, usually precipitated by Mike. While in a hurry, Mike forgot to set the parking brake in his car. The car rolled into the neighbor's new Cadillac and they had a huge bill for damages. Another time he was distracted by a beautiful view and forgot to watch his step. He fell twisting his ankle and was on crutches (and out of work) for six weeks. Each time Jane rescues Mike.

She tells me that she stays very busy: "There are bills to be paid; I have to concentrate on making money." And "I've made commitments; I can't disappoint people who depend on me." At other times she says, "I do everything right." She is angry and frustrated that doing everything right hasn't led to happiness or peace for her. She has learned all the rules and she follows them exactly. She tries hard.

I agree with her, saying: "It's not fair. You do everything expected of you. Others probably aren't as careful as you are." We acknowledge that her way of being good isn't bringing her peace and conclude that "doing" must be irrelevant to personal satisfaction. Otherwise, she would have everything she wants.

Doing isn't the path and peace isn't a goal to be achieved – peace is a process, a way of being every moment. When I ask Jane to take twenty minutes to sit and do nothing, she becomes noticeably agitated. Adamantly she states that she cannot "do nothing." Doing nothing for her is watching television or working a crossword puzzle. I ask her to describe her fantasy of what would happen if she were to do nothing. After a pause, she describes an image of a building falling apart around her, leaving her stuck in rubble while dust hangs in the air. When I ask her how she is freed from the "stuckness" in her image, she replies that since she can do nothing, she remains stuck. Remaining stuck, she dies.

Being active and busy insures Jane's survival in her own mind. She has always been effective in saving herself and Mike. When she can overcome adversity, she benefits. She feels rewarded as the One Who Shoulders the World's Burdens. As long as she has a project to work on, she can contain her anxiety and fear, shoving them aside for the moment. That way she can "manage" her feelings. She doesn't feel them very intensely and they don't interfere with her accomplishments. As long as she can prove to herself that she can solve any problem, she feels comforted. Temporarily.

Jane needs to continually prove to herself that she will survive because basically she fears that she won't. As a child she didn't learn to trust that someone capable would protect her. In fact, she learned that the comings and goings of those around her were unpredictable. She wasn't told, at the age of three, that her father was deploying with his Navy division for a year. She gradually and fearfully discovered that her protector was absent. "OK," she must have told herself as a child, "If no one will protect me, I'll protect myself. I'll stay away from hurt feelings. I'll act as if they don't exist."

As an adult Jane has used work to avoid vulnerability. She believed that she couldn't "do" anything about her fear of loss, her anxiety about survival, or her uncertainty about being loved. She also thought that she couldn't tolerate the pain of those feelings. But she could work hard. She focused her attention on work to hide her fears and her doubts.

Before she married Mike, Jane wondered if anyone would ever love her; she feared that she might be alone forever. This thought terrified her. So, of course, she jumped at the chance to be married. Maybe Mike drank excessively and abused drugs, but at least she could be Mrs. Somebody Else. That seemed to still some of the demons who tormented her with accusations of unworthiness. Temporarily.

The first five years of their marriage were a "nightmare." She described Mike as being "out of control." He was arrested for drunk driving, he received speeding tickets, and he might or might not come home each night. So, because her unconscious had already decided what to do in difficult situations, Jane focused her attention on working and on saving Mike from the predicaments he created. Over and over again, Jane rescued him.

When Mike would create crises, Jane would muster her strength. When he was consumed with the volatility of his life, she would be steady. She received no emotional support from Mike and very little help financially.

After five years of marriage, Mike quit drinking and went to Alcoholics Anonymous. A few months later, Jane started attending Al-Anon meetings. She relinquished her more obvious rescues and their life together became somewhat calmer.

The fact that Mike didn't support her was, in a convoluted sense, comfortable for Jane. It reinforced her belief that "you can't count on anyone." She had learned to deny her needs for comfort and nurturing and someone to lean on while she was still young. She continued her denial with Mike. With so much excitement outside of her, she couldn't afford to look inside and to feel the deep wounds there. Mike offered her a compelling distraction from her inner world.

Without trying, Jane had developed a marriage relationship which mirrored the relationship between her prominent subpersonalities. She identified with her Controller while she denied and projected her vulnerable Child feelings onto Mike.

Mike represented a part of Jane that she didn't want to see. Inside of her was pain and fear, while outside she maintained an appearance of total control. She didn't look into her inner world. She feared that her feelings would overwhelm her control and she believed that survival depended upon maintaining a strong Controller. By refusing to acknowledge her vulnerable parts – her disappointments, her neediness, her hurts, and her fears – she created a reality in which they would be shown to her. She couldn't avoid it. She had to see outside of her in Mike what she didn't want to see inside of her.

Couples are together because they have something to learn from each other. One reflects the other's hidden, unconscious parts. If there is some quality that irks you and you don't want to see it in yourself, you'll be shown it in your mate or someone else in your life. We are all here to help each other become clearer in our consciousness through this process of recognizing our projections.

Who gets to you? Who can you really not stand? What qualities does that person manifest that you're refusing to see in yourself? What is the value of having that person in your life? (Yes, there is value. You need to see him/her so as to know yourself. If you don't want to know someone else, what is it in *you* that you don't want to know?)

There's no sense blaming your mate. You drew him/her into your life. So when you're annoyed with him/her, look inside yourself for some unacceptable subpersonality who hasn't been heard. As long as Jane focused her attention on Mike and not on her hurt Child, she could not heal, and therefore nothing in her life could change significantly.

You have a basic responsibility to heal your inner world. And only *your* inner world. When you acknowledge this fact, you learn clearly and strongly the Universal Law of Non-Interference: **If it's not your life, don't try to live it**. You won't have time to manage someone else's affairs if you truly take responsibility for your own. If you do have time and energy to choreograph another's every movement, you are probably not giving your inner world all the attention it deserves.

As we attend to our needs and wounds internally, we notice consistencies with our outer world experience. We notice that the husband we have chosen elicits in us the same reactions we felt early in life with a parent. Dependency with him works out the same way that dependency with a parent did. If we didn't receive much understanding from a parent, we probably won't receive much from a mate.

If our needs were treated with care in childhood, we learned to respect our needs. We identify with our parents and unconsciously form our own caring internal Parent. Then we project that Caring Parent onto a mate. But the essential middle step is the internal subpersonality we have developed and for which we are responsible.

Jane had developed a Controller who treated her Child as insensitively as her parents had. Not surprisingly, she hooked up with a mate who didn't acknowledge her needs and feelings, either. What else could happen? If gentleness doesn't already exist inside, it can't take form outside.

Conceiving a child was the only goal in Jane's life with which her Controller couldn't aid her. Thus, it was in this arena that she would have to look into her Shadow – her vulnerability, her needs, and her fears. Acknowledging her feeling world was a 180 degree shift for Jane.

Finally willing to look inside, Jane followed her imagery. She saw her Controller as a thick steel wall. Nothing could get through the highly polished Controller wall or dent it. Very effectively, it prevented Jane's fearful Child from being seen or heard. Jane imagined the Child to be untouchably isolated behind the Controller wall. The impenetrable wall insured that the hurting, fearful Child would never embarrass the Controller, but it also prevented the Child from healing.

Living behind that wall, the Child believed that no one would ever help her. In fact, no one could. The Controller prohibited any caring from penetrating through to the Child. The Child felt hopelessly alone and ignored behind the wall.

When we talked about Jane re-establishing a relationship with the Child, she hesitated. "There is so much pain; I don't want to feel it all." At the same time,

Jane expressed a longing to be complete, a sense that some essential part of her was missing. She was trying to give herself something new from the outside (a baby) to, hopefully, make herself feel better rather than relating to that hidden inner Child and allowing healing to happen from within through the relationship.

Haven't we all been taught that taking in something from outside us – food, another person's attention, alcohol, clothes, toys, TV – will make us feel better? The answer is always "out there" and we have to chase it. But Jane had done that long enough, and now she was willing to consider the inner journey I suggested.

So, Jane decided to become acquainted with her Child even though she was afraid. (After all, when had she let her feelings dissuade her once she had made a decision?) She first looked to see what the Child was doing. "She's a quiet girl, playing by herself, wondering what she is supposed to do next." Her Child was so accustomed to being jerked around, following her "shoulds," that she couldn't easily tell Jane what she wanted. She exhibited no spontaneity. After watching her for many moments, Jane asked the girl what she was feeling. "I want you to love me," the Child said.

Jane realized that the girl was looking for acceptance. Again, she hesitated. Intuitively, Jane knew that accepting the Child involved a major commitment. She couldn't fool the girl as she could fool the adults in her outside world. The Child would know if she were truly present to her. Jane's experience had been that other adults were satisfied with a good show and she knew how to give them that. But she couldn't keep emotional distance from the girl.

Commitment to that inner Child meant that Jane would have to let go of her choice to not feel. Commitment to that Child meant that Jane would feel everything that Child was feeling. She had lived since childhood with her decision to block off feelings. Could she totally reverse that decision?

Jane wasn't sure that she could or that she wanted to. She feared embarrassing herself in front of co-workers, crying in public, and exploding with anger at her parents. Doing any of these things would upset the control Jane had constructed in her world. She might lose all of her relationships and the respect of her acquaintances.

When Jane was expressing her fears she realized that she was identified with her Controller, that these were the Controller's fears. When Jane remembered that she was both the Controller and the Child, she could allow herself to step back and to hear from each of them without taking sides. She heard:

Controller: I've built a comfortable life. I have a good job and earn decent money. My home is lovely and people who know me respect me. You might destroy all that I've worked so hard to build.

Child: I'm not comfortable. I'm not happy. I feel like you only want to ignore me. You're afraid that I might smash your world.

Controller: Yes, that's what I'm afraid of. I would prefer that you didn't exist at all. If I could kill you and be free of your depression, I would. I've tried.

Child: You have managed to keep me away from you. You've isolated me. I don't make myself known very often but you can't kill this pain over not conceiving. It doesn't matter what you say, I feel the ache because biologically I will never be a mother.

Controller: You have your pets. The world doesn't need any more children anyway.

Child: (sobs hysterically)

Jane did not know how to move beyond this impasse. Her usual approach – reasoning – was useless. The fight between her Controller and Child could not be resolved rationally nor would it disappear on its own. This scene was replayed regularly with the Controller maintaining prominence until the intensity of the Child's feelings overwhelmed the Controller. Then there would be sobbing. When the crying had diminished, again the Controller was on top and the cycle continued.

But Jane knew that there must be a way for her subpersonalities to relate to each other differently. She called upon an inner Adult figure to speak to the Controller.

Adult: While I would like to be perfect and to not have uncomfortable feelings, I do feel a huge lack in my life. The joy is missing. I want to be whole. I want to acknowledge the Child and listen to her.

Controller: I will allow you to listen to her here in the therapy office, but I don't want you to share her with your friends.

Jane's Adult agreed to this condition. With the Controller willing to temporarily withdraw, Jane wanted the Child to speak about herself, but Jane needed a Caring Parent to be there, a figure who could respond to the Child's feelings as well as to the Adult's rationality.

In her imagery Jane invited a Caring Parent to come. She didn't receive a picture as much as an encompassing feeling of warmth and love and welcome for the Child. When the Caring Parent became prominent in Jane her cheeks flushed a bit and she said, "I have never felt my heart open so fully. I am ready to receive the Child. Already I cherish her."

And she saw the Caring Parent and the Child come together. The Child was slow to speak. She whispered so that the Parent had to strain to hear her:

Child: My feelings are so big. I can't feel all of them all by myself. Parent: I know. I'm here with you.

Child: But you won't stay long.

Parent: I'll be here with you as long as I can. When I have to go I promise I will return. I won't ignore you.

Child: I'm going to die. I can't stand these feelings. Parent: Let me hold you. I'm here.

Child: The pain will kill me.

Parent: I'll protect you. No one will take away your life. I love you and I will watch over you.

Child: I'm afraid.

Parent: I know. Your feelings scare you. They're big and they're awful. But I'll be here with you while you feel them. Just look up at me every once in a while and remember that I'm here holding you. I won't let go of you.

Child: Please don't leave me. I can't make it on my own. I need you. Parent: I understand. I'll be here for you as long as you need me.

Child: What if you have to go?

Parent: I will be back. I won't leave you on your own for very long. You're too little to survive without my protection and I will protect you. So, just go ahead and cry all you want and hurt until the hurt is gone. I'll be here.

Child: Don't go away. I need you. Parent: You have me.

Through her Caring Parent Jane listened to the Child talk about her fear, loneliness, alienation, and self-doubt. The Child became aware of, and grateful for, the Parent's concern. As she cried in the Parent's arms, she healed. After an hour of sobbing with fear and alienation, the Child felt stronger and closer to the Parent who didn't abandon her. This experience was repeated frequently for weeks.

As the Child realized that she wouldn't be silenced again, her loneliness changed. "Loneliness" was the word the Child used to describe her feelings when she couldn't connect with the Caring Parent part of Jane. Jane had involved herself in all kinds of groups but her loneliness had not healed just by contact with other people. It was only when the Parent welcomed the Child with concern and a willingness to listen that the Child felt relief from her loneliness.

The Child experienced acceptance of her feelings and vulnerability from the Parent's attention and as she did, they lessened. Her feelings weren't terrifying or overwhelming. The Caring Parent certainly could handle hearing them.

Jane hadn't developed her Caring Parent subpersonality prior to therapy because she had never had a model for that part of her. Her Controller had been modelled for her when she was a child, so she related to her inner Child from her Controller. When I showed her another way of relating to her feelings, she could replicate that model and develop her inner Caring Parent. First she had projected that figure onto me. Then she owned her projection and found the Caring Parent inside of her.

Jane wrote in her journal at this time:

> However my Child feels in relation to the Caring Parent seems to be my experience in the world. When the Child feels safe with the Parent, I feel safe in the world. When the Child trusts that the Parent cares about her needs, I find myself trusting that others will treat my needs with respect. As my Parent nurtures my Child and protects her, I find that somehow I receive emotional and financial support, especially from Mike. Whatever goes on between my subpersonalities, especially those two, is reproduced in the outer world.

The most amazing change I've noticed has been in relation to Mike. When I started therapy, he didn't understand what I was looking for. He didn't want to participate directly and, after the first couple of months, I saw that the problems really weren't between us but in my way of thinking. (Not that he didn't contribute his share of craziness!) So, I didn't pressure him to change or make him responsible for my happiness. I just focused on my inner world. (I never knew there was so much going on inside me.) I had always been responsible for keeping everything in order around me; I didn't realize that I was irresponsible about not attending to the confusion inside me. There was a whole world of hidden feelings there, feelings I really didn't want to see.

Specifically, my Child was the part of me that I had always, without knowing I was doing it, hidden. I kept her behind the Wall. When I was three or four, I couldn't do anything else but hide all my pain and outrage. My fears of dying as a result of being abandoned were crippling. Of course, I couldn't handle them when I was a kid. I didn't have my Caring Parent then. The abandoned Child was just left on her own to try to survive however she could. She couldn't, really, by herself, so my Controller removed her from all those awful feelings which threatened to destroy her by erecting that Wall to hide the fears and the pain.

Unconsciously, I must have recognized my abandoned Child in Mike when I met him. He's just like her in so many ways! He's angry and confused and in so much pain. When I first met him, something in me was pulled to him. I didn't know what it was – certainly relating to him was difficult; he just would not do what I knew was good for him! I tried so hard to get him to straighten out. The hassles we had! But in Al-Anon, and especially in therapy, I learned where my responsibility lay – with my Child inside. I hadn't even realized I had a part of me like her.

So I started to do for her what I had tried to do for Mike. Just being with her was painful. I hated experiencing all those old feelings – the fear and the desperation. But that's what having a relationship with someone is about, feeling whatever they're feeling with them. So I did it. I could only share her pain by finding the part of me that wasn't needy, that had an inner source of strength. All these years when I've acted so strong it was a cover-up; I was pretending. I didn't even know there was another way to live. I thought that since life was hard, I had to be tough.

I realized by listening to the Child that what I was missing was gentleness. That's always what I've loved about Mike. He's outrageous and embarrassing, but there is such a large part of him that is tender and sweet. Now I see how much I needed that in my life and how I wanted him to give it to me.

So without knowing it, I had made an unspoken agreement with him – I would take care of his needs for worldy security and he would provide me the feelings I had lost. But the more intense his feelings were, the more I tried to control them and him. That's how I had always handled my own feelings. It was only when I learned a different way of relating to feelings in therapy that I could have a different relationship with Mike. Sometimes I marvel that our marriage could have survived all those tumultuous, chaotic years. We were kids when we got together and committed ourselves to each other. We didn't know what we were doing. Or did we? Actually, we couldn't have been more perfect for each other. That's why we drove each other nuts!

As my Caring Parent introduced gentleness into the relationship with my Child, I must have changed in relation to Mike, because he is more sensitive and more responsible towards me now. I let him live his own life without (too much) interference from me and he does just fine. He's had some blows, but he recovered from them and learned his lessons.

He seems to be experiencing a shift in his inner relationships between his Demanding Child and his Responsible Adult. When I finally got out of his way, his Responsible Adult strengthened and related to the Demanding Child out of that strength. In the past, I had prevented that relationship from developing by always overwhelming his Adult. I could be more responsible, sooner and faster, so his Responsible Adult didn't have a chance.

When I backed off and related to my own hurting Child instead of to his, he could develop more balance inside of himself. And he seems to be truly pleased with himself for doing that. He's more independent and self-confident and his job performance is more reliable than ever. He's apparently enjoying his stability even more than the thrills of previous years. He acts more whole and more adult. Coming from that strong place, he has more support to offer me and seems glad to do so.

A year after therapy ended I visited Jane in her home. She and Mike had just adopted a baby boy and were thrilled. She told me that when she committed herself to relating to her inner Child, her desperate need for a baby vanished. When her wish for a baby assumed normal proportions, when it wasn't based on denial or fear of her own feelings, it was fulfilled. She did her inside work and her outside situation fell into place without effort.

How do you treat your Needy Child?

Do you ignore his/her needs? Do you indulge them?

Do you tell yourself that other people's wants are more important than your inner Child's needs?

Describe your Controller in terms of what s/he says to you. How does s/he want you to act?

If it were up to your Controller, what image would you project?

If your Child were to be seen as s/he is, what image would you project?

Listen to your Controller and your Child having a dialogue. Write what you hear.

Now have the same dialogue between the Child and a gentle Caring Parent. Again, write what you hear.

EXERCISE

Imagine yourself sitting and watching a glass elevator. The elevator is on the level above you but is descending. Inside the elevator is your Child. As the elevator descends notice the Child's feet and lower legs. (Pause) Then notice the upper legs and torso. (Pause) As the elevator continues to descend, notice the Child's upper body, arms, and head. (Pause)

The elevator reaches your level and stops. The doors open but the Child remains in the elevator. Notice the facial expression, the body posture, and the breathing of the Child. (Pause) Have the Child verbalize a statement about him/herself. (Pause) Slowly the elevator doors close and the Child is carried to a higher level.

Continue watching. Again the elevator descends. This time your Parent is in it. Notice the Parent's feet, lower legs, upper legs, manner of dress, torso, arms, neck, and face. (Pause) The elevator doors open. Notice the body posture, facial expression, and breathing pattern of the Parent. (Pause) Have the Parent make a statement about him/herself and just listen. (Pause) Again the elevator doors close and the figure is carried to a higher level.

Continue watching. This time the elevator descends with both the Child and the Parent in it. Watch as the elevator approaches your level. See the doors open. (Pause) Notice the body postures of the two figures. (Pause) Notice if they are touching each other or interacting in any way. (Pause) Have the Child turn to the Parent and say something – express a feeling or ask a question. The Child can say anything at all that s/he wants. S/he may communicate non-verbally or verbally. (Pause) Notice how the Parent receives the Child's message. (Pause) Does s/he respond? (Pause) How? (Pause) Does the communication between them continue? (Pause) Does the Parent ask the Child for something? What do you notice about their relationship as they interact? (Pause) What seems to be the feeling tone between them? (Pause)

Have their communication continue as long as you want. (Pause) When they conclude, notice if they touch. (Pause) What is the feeling in the scene you are watching? (Pause)

The elevator doors close and the elevator ascends. Watch the Child and the Parent until they are no longer in view. What is happening in your body now? (Pause) How deeply are you breathing?

REFLECTIONS

Describe your imagery.

What did you notice about the Parent? The Child? Their relationship? How is this dynamic enacted in your life and relationships?

When do you identify with your Parent? How do you act then? What do you say? What do you appreciate about your Parent? When do you identify with your Child?

How do you act then? What do you say? What do you appreciate about your Child?

What do the Parent and Child appreciate about each other? What do the Parent and Child want from each other?

What is your reaction to your imagery? Write any thoughts that come to mind.

Chapter 6

RELATIONSHIPS ARE REFLECTIONS

At thirty-nine, Beth was a successful professional woman with a neat, business-like appearance. Everything about her was conservative – her dress, her manner, her speech, her hairstyle. She added few "frivolous touches" to enhance her natural good looks. She used very little make-up and wore long skirts, usually black or navy. She spoke in softly modulated tones, but her forehead was often furrowed and her shoulders held high. Her body bespoke tension.

Beth stated that she could handle herself competently and assertively in business contacts with men but that she felt frustrated in personal relationships when her feelings and wants were involved. She said that she wanted to be with a man who understood her, who was sensitive to her feelings. And with a sigh she added, "But that's never happened. Not for very long. Most of the time I tell myself to forget it, but really, in my heart and soul, that's what I want." She sighed again and studied her hands.

Although Beth initially presented a facade that was completely rational – her thoughts organized and her life planned – when she talked about relationships she spoke with uncertainty. She took off her glasses and laid them on the small table by her chair. Her eyes were surprisingly expressive when they were unshielded, welling with tears as she described her disappointments and frustrations in love relationships.

"When things don't work for me I identify the problem and take action to correct it. So, in this area I tried the little things first – new clothes, a new haircut, a dating service. I even tried to shed a few pounds." She smirked as though she recognized the silliness of these attempts. "But none of those things made any difference." She looked down again and though I could not see her eyes I could feel her embarrassment and confusion.

It was as though Beth were operating on two parallel tracks. Professionally, her skills led her to accomplishment and acclaim. Personally, the same skills couldn't save her from loneliness. I realized that I was responding to two subpersonalities. On the one hand, her "bottom line" Business Woman, her more noticeable subpersonality, encouraged efficiency. "Time is money," the Business Woman seemed to be saying, "so let's not waste any."

Her "Let's-take-care-of-business" subpersonality contrasted sharply with the other side of her, the one who had led her into therapy. This second subpersonality was a Confused Child, retiring and afraid. The Child had no sense of being in charge of her life and no understanding of why things were the way they were. She seemed to stumble from one feeling into another without recognizing patterns in her relationships. Beth's brown eyes softened when she identified with the Confused Child.

Unconsciously, Beth was looking for balance in the out of balance status quo that these two very unequal subpersonalities maintained. She wanted a man to compensate for the lack of emotional development of her Child.

She had worked very hard for fourteen years and had achieved unusual success in her career. Now her work required less attention. The tension within her, pulling her towards relationship grew, but Beth didn't know how to respond to her inner changes. Her professional skills were of no value when feelings were involved.

For several weeks, we focused on differentiating these two figures. Beth knew the Business Woman well. She verbalized her values about logic, rationality, and smooth management easily. Indeed, she usually identified with the Business Woman. She thought that the Business Woman's approach to life was the only respectable way to live.

The loneliness Beth had experienced provided the impetus to examine her retiring subpersonality, the Child. Beth had never given much prominence to the Confused Child and, consequently, she didn't know her. The Child is the part of us involved in relationships. In the first part of our lives we engage in relationships in order to meet our needs for love and security – the same needs we had when we were born. We unconsciously structure our lives so that the way these needs were met in our young lives is repeated later in life. If dependency wasn't safe as a child, you need to help your hurt Child recover by allowing the Child to fully feel her disappointment or sadness and by holding him/her while s/he cries. Only when the inner dependency needs are met, can a dependency relationship with another person work out well.

Beth had learned to think logically as a way of denying her feelings when she was a child. Her parents were intellectually oriented and any problem which came up was subject to intellectual scrutiny. It was dissected, analyzed, discussed. Feelings, too, were subjected to this process. Then they were dismissed as being inferior to a cognitive way of living. Thus, early in life, Beth developed an analytical subpersonality and denied her Confused Child as she imitated her parents.

It was only now in therapy when Beth was accepting the Confused Child's right to her own existence that she could listen to this smaller subpersonality. She heard her Child say:

I am unbearably lonely. When Friday afternoon comes and I know I will be alone for two days, I'm frightened and sad. I don't know what to do. I walk around the park or go to the zoo and everywhere I see happy couples, men and women holding on to each other and laughing. It looks wonderful to me; that's what I want. I want it desperately but I don't know how to get it.

Beth noticed how the Confused Child felt overwhelmed and helpless while the Business Woman was always in charge of her life. These two subpersonalities represented very different energies in Beth, two sides to her that seemed to have nothing in common besides living in the same body.

Two months after she had begun therapy, Beth met Sam. Within two weeks he had moved in with her. He provided the nurturing and understanding she had wanted. They talked for hours. He empathized with her in a way no other man had. He attended to her wants. (Since he wasn't working, he had few distractions.) He made her feelings the center of their conversations. Beth said that she was transformed, that she had never experienced such fulfillment. Her Child was sure this was the Prince who would save her from misery and confusion.

Three months later Sam disappeared as quickly as he had appeared. Beth was devastated. She again felt her old loneliness. "Why doesn't love work? How did I ruin this relationship? What am I doing that's so wrong?" Her Child's confusion grew and her feelings of inadequacy were confirmed.

The Confused Child asked these questions repeatedly each time a relationship had ended. Ever since she was an adolescent, this pattern had periodically led Beth into deep depressions. When she was dating someone, she was energetic, active, and hopeful. When each relationship ended she withdrew, spent most of her time indoors, and gained weight. The Confused Child said, "If I can't be loved by a man, I'll give myself love by eating. It's one way not to hurt so much." As far as relationships went (when she was open to them), Beth was either imagining herself about to be lifted out of her lifelong disappointments or plummeting down a dark hole, bereft of hope, overcome by ever-returning despair. The Business Woman avoided the whole area of relationships and focused on work. It was possible for her to be successful at work; relationships only led to unhappiness.

After the Confused Child had been prominent in each relationship and each had ended so miserably, the Business Woman reasserted herself. At least *she* knew how to be successful. She was so angry with the Confused Child for creating yet another debacle that she would resume prominence and block the Child out. So again, Beth's energy would be funnelled into work and the Child's needs for love pushed out of awareness.

After several months of self-imposed isolation, with her Business Woman completely ignoring the Confused Child, Beth's loneliness and need for companionship would again fuel the Child's restlessness. Then, using the Child's judgment, Beth would jump into a relationship with any man. The cycle would repeat.

With Sam's departure, Beth recognized her pain as being a panicky fear of death. Her Adult mind told her that she wasn't helpless, but her feelings seemed to come from an Abandoned Infant. That Infant thought that if her chosen source of nurturance (in this case Sam) was not attending to her she wouldn't survive. With this insight Beth realized that she was experiencing more than the disappointment of losing another adult relationship. She was also reliving some earlier unresolved feelings. The Abandoned Infant was at the core of her Confused Child. The dependency and the disappointment in the relationship with Sam were similar to her childhood pains. The current situation reawakened the buried Abandoned Infant and her terrified feelings.

Previously, when these painful feelings of abandonment had arisen at the end of a relationship, Beth had always pushed them away. She had felt afraid and overwhelmed by their intensity. Her Business Woman would take over and the wound buried, unhealed because the feelings had not been fully felt. But now, being older, feeling stronger in general, and having the framework for understanding her experience that therapy provided, Beth listened to the Abandoned Infant. She wrote in her journal:

> The Abandoned Infant in me is wailing. She's a baby and she's terrified. Somehow she's been left alone. She knows she was with her mother at one time but somehow her mother disappeared. She doesn't know why. She only knows that she can't make it on her own. Her cries are pleas to be noticed, to be picked up, hopefully, to be held. Without her mother's protection the Infant fears she will die.

She wails and screams for someone to notice her but her screams are swallowed by the darkness. She learns that she is truly alone, isolated in the most basic way. And she wasn't alone just a week ago, maybe just a day ago. What changed? She didn't. She was loved and she expected the love to continue. But it disappeared. And now she's lost. This isn't her world and she doesn't know how to survive in this strange scary place.

The aloneness is too much for such a little baby. She can't feed herself and she can't comfort herself and she can't make herself safe. Where is mom? Everything this baby had counted on has disappeared and she doesn't know how or why or exactly when. She is overcome with absolute abject bone-chilling terror. She is sure to die unless someone rescues her.

Her terror grows. No one is there to hold her, no one even hears her. She didn't always feel this way and she knows this isn't right. She has to find a protector. She can't survive unless someone loves her. Death is very real in her untouchable isolation. She can't connect to anyone. Not to anyone at all. What will it take for her to get someone's attention? She has to get someone to notice her. If no one thinks about her she will perish. She will disappear and no one will notice.

Re-experiencing her terror, Beth sobbed through much of the first month after Sam's departure. She described nightmares which woke her at least once a night. She lost ten pounds; since she wasn't resisting her feelings, she didn't choose to eat unless her body needed food. She felt miserable but she didn't fight her feelings. She trusted that by feeling them she was healing.

As she spent time with her inner world and knew her moods more precisely, she identified the Critic, the subpersonality who, she now realized, had influenced her for years. Beth recognized that the Critic's voice was loud and punishing. As Beth listened to the Critic's words, she recognized familiar condemnations and thoughts she had had about her own lack of value when each relationship had ended. She wrote in her journal:

> Dealing with the Critic inside of me has been difficult. For years I didn't hear her voice clearly or recognize that her criticisms weren't true. I only knew I was depressed. I think that voice has been with me since I was young, but I've used food, alcohol, television, and work to avoid it.

The Critic wants to kill me. She hates me, disparages me, and wants to hurt me any way she can. She tells me that no one loves me and that no one could love me because I'm such a horrible person. She tells me I'm fat and repulsive, that no one could stand being around me. She points out mistakes I make and ridicules me for them. So, of course I've wanted to avoid the Critic. I guess I hoped a lover would silence that voice forever, but it never worked. I couldn't avoid her.

I was displeased about my relationships, but they were just a reflection of my inner conflict with the Critic. That was where the real action was – inside my head. Funny how that's always available to work on – I can't go anywhere without my head – and yet I try to avoid it. The Critic's words frighten me. There is such power in them. The Critic scares me as though she were real and large and looming outside my body, threatening to hurt me. The danger seems great and imminent. The power seems not to be mine, but to belong to an enemy. She seems to be something autonomous inside of me which isn't me, and yet, she obviously *is* a part of me. I just can't get rid of her or integrate her.

I guess the Critic/Child interaction is the 'primary relationship' inside of me which isn't working – a prototype for all my external relationships. There's no hope of anything going smoothly outside until I deal with the Critic. No one can save me from her.

The Critic is as real a person as anyone I can see or touch. I hear her voice when I am still. I know when to listen for her by noticing my behavior. If I start to do anything compulsively – eating, working, exercising – I know the Critic is at work and I'm trying to block her out. My anxiety about being alone is a sure giveaway that I am afraid of being with her. Such a tyrant to have attached to me!

I can't really escape the Critic, although I've tried to tell her off and take control. Since that didn't work, I'm going to call upon an Adult part of me to listen to her.

Adult: I can feel how angry you are, Critic. I know you hate me.

Critic: You're right. I do. Wouldn't anyone?

Adult: Some people don't. Some people like me.

Critic: They don't know you the way I do. If they really saw you in your truth instead of that act you put on, they would treat you the same way I do.

Adult: Maybe. But some of them have seen me at my worst and they've never said to me the things you say. I want to die after you've spoken to me.

Critic: That's because I tell you the truth. You deserve to be dead.

Adult: (What can I say to that? She's my enemy and wants to stay that way.) Critic, you are so angry. You must be very hurt. No one has treated you very well if you treat me this way.

Critic: I know what you're doing and it won't work. Sure, I've been alone all my life. That's how life is. You're a sissy believing it's otherwise. You're just too weak to make it.

Adult: You seem very strong to me. How did you become so strong?

Critic: Through feeling hurt and then realizing that I had to get tough. If I wasn't tough, I would be just like you – a wimp – always simpering, falling apart at the slightest blow. And *I* wouldn't live that way. You may not have standards for how you appear to others, but I do and I won't conduct myself in such a needy fashion.

Adult: No, you've never appeared needy or wimpy to me.

Critic: Well, I'm not. I can't allow that. I can't afford to think only about my feelings. I have work to do. I want to be a grown-up in this world so I act like one.

Adult: You do appear to be grown up.

Critic: And don't try to dig any deeper. That's all there is. Adult: I want to be grown up, too, but I still have needs.

Critic: That's because you're such a wimp. You've got to stop always thinking about your feelings. Just get rid of them.

Adult: Have you ever had anyone really love you?

Critic: It doesn't matter.

Adult: It's always mattered to me.

Critic: I can't afford the luxury of wallowing in feelings like you do.

Adult: I understand how that wouldn't fit for you. I would like to get to know you. You've obviously done some thinking and have worked out your life in your own way.

Critic: And if you'd listen to me you could do the same thing.
Adult: I'm listening.

Critic: I can't see that you've found a secret that I haven't. I know that no one is going to take care of you. You might as well give up hoping and trying to make it so.

Adult: Did you want to be taken care of at one time?

Critic: Sure, but I got over it. It's too painful to keep re-hashing that neediness the way you do. I couldn't put up with that much pain. It interferes with my efficiency.

Adult: It probably scared you, too.

Critic: I don't remember feeling scared, but I didn't want to live that way, so I just made up my mind and I changed those feelings.

Adult: Mind over feelings.

Critic: Yes and it works.

Adult: Do you overeat or stay busy?

Critic: What's that got to do with anything? Adult: Don't you see that they are related?

Critic: Efficiency and eating are two different things.

Adult: Sometimes, do you feel more cravings to eat than at other times?

Critic: Are you trying to get into my head now? If I feel like eating more sometimes, it's just physical. Don't introduce all that psychological garbage.

Adult: I respect all the things you've been able to get done. Certainly your efficiency has paid off and been recognized.

Critic: Right. So when are you going to get with it?

Adult: I don't know if I can function that way anymore. I used to be able to pull it off for short periods, but I can't continue that cycle. So, I will accept that you have your answers and I will accept me and keep looking for mine. I may always be searching.

Critic: If that's how you want to live. . . . I don't know why anyone would choose that way, always struggling. Why not just settle it and get on with the business of life?

Adult: I don't know how to answer that question. I just have to do what comes from inside me. I can't cut myself off from my needs and still be me and be alive and do what I have to do. Maybe we are each living in our own way but we are just very different.

Critic: Maybe. I don't understand you and I'm not really interested. Just don't come crying to me when you're in pain. If you've chosen to continue feeling your feelings, you will feel pain sometimes too, so don't expect that I will solve that for you.

Adult: OK, you've got a deal. I hope we can still talk sometimes. I admit that I don't understand you and I don't expect you to understand me, but I think I would like to continue knowing you.

Critic: I'll be here. I just wish you'd take care of yourself.

Beth's Critic, a subpersonality she had formed unconsciously when she was a child based on childhood impressions of successful adults, was now her own internal living figure. The Critic, modeled on Beth's parents, had all the same qualities as the Business Woman – rationality, logic, clarity, but she was also furiously angry with Beth's child and condemning of her whenever the Child was present.

The Business Woman was just a specific form of the Critic which Beth found useful in her outer life. The Critic had tried to silence the Child's feelings and had dominated Beth by encouraging Beth's identification with the Business Woman. Beth had always experienced an intense conflict between her Critic and her Child but due to the Business Woman's prominence and her denial of the Child, Beth was unaware of what her tension reflected. It hadn't seemed that there was another part to her other than the Business Woman – there were just unexplainable depressions and weight gain. She had thought that truly the Business Woman was all there was to her. Now she could clearly identify her Child's needs and hear her Critic's voice. Listening to the Critic kept Beth from being overrun by her. Beth found that she had to offer the Critic exactly what she (Beth) wanted to receive: acceptance. By allowing the Critic to be angry with her and by listening to that anger, Beth had formed a relationship with the Critic. Knowing the Critic involved being able to see her clearly. Just as intimacy with another person requires that we respect each other's separateness and boundaries, so does intimacy between subpersonalities. Getting to know one subpersonality is like getting to know any person. Each has a history, her own values, and her own way of thinking.

When Beth's Adult and Critic were talking and listening to each other, her Child didn't get depressed. As long as they could talk and listen to one another, the punishment from the Critic was eliminated. Like an intrapsychic United Nations, with more talk there were fewer battles.

Beth's angry Critic didn't disappear altogether, though. She was still aware that the Critic was active when she felt depressed, unloved, and alone. At those times her Adult stepped in front of the Child and listened and talked with the Critic. After several months of internal conversations, she recognized that it wasn't only the Critic who was angry. The Child was also upset.

Adult: I feel intense anger. Who is there?

Child: When you didn't say anything to my co-worker, Kim, to stop her from hurting me, my feeling of being powerless returned. You are the voice through which I have power. If you don't speak for me I am totally powerless. I need you to protect me and to define my limits for others.

Adult: I was caught off guard last week. I will be prepared next time. I tried to protect you with Julie last month. I think your voice came through too much, though, way too loudly.

Child: But at least you tried to protect me. I knew you heard me and acknowledged me. You were supportive of me. If you listen to me and take care of me and don't try to make me disappear, I don't feel rage. It's you I react to, not Julie or Kim or anyone else out there. They are just being themselves, but you won't let me be myself. You seem so concerned about making space for everyone else, but you squelch me. Why do I have to be sacrificed so that everyone else can be happy? Why do you care so much about them and apparently nothing about me? I won't allow you to ignore me. I am truly dependent upon your voice.

Adult: I can see that now. I will lend my voice to your needs but you scare me with your intensity. I guess that's why I worry about what you will say to people. We need a Moderator so that we can communicate with each other and with the outside world, too.

Moderator: Adult, you tuned the Child out for a long time because she had tantrums. Now she is more mature. She can explain herself and you can understand her. I want her to be heard. I want to insure that her anger is recognized. We must consider with whom we are speaking. Kim is young and doesn't know her own inner world. She is flailing. She may be near her bottom point, so we have to remember that her stress is already extreme.

Child: Are you forgetting about me?

Moderator: No, I just want you to understand the situation you are going into. There are considerations other than your needs. We've seen what happens when you think only of yourself – other people are hurt and you are still unhappy. I am aware that in the past the Adult has concentrated on others and excluded you. I can understand why you would be tense when you hear me talking that way, too. I want to take care of you, but I want to be your intermediary with others, also. I can't totally give in to you. I hear your concerns and I respect them, but I respect other people's needs, also. Kim, as a person, has a need not to be belittled or hurt. She is projecting onto everyone. It's obvious that she isn't solid. However, she is still responsible for her behavior. We will have to let her know her limits and what is unacceptable. I will do that. She has intense energy but no focus or understanding. I will offer her a channel for directing her energy and I will protect you.

Child: OK, just don't forget me.

Moderator: I promise I never will. When I am in charge I want to hear your voice. But I will have the last word. I will own the needs you present to me and I will commit to staying open to you. I will help your feelings find a forum which will be heard and which won't increase your isolation.

Child: OK. I don't completely trust you yet, but I will give your proposal a chance.

Beth's Moderator, an impartial mediator, reclaimed the Child's needs and expressed them through her own voice. The Moderator had not been a prominent part of Beth up to that point in her life. The struggle between the Critic and the Child had intensely consumed most of Beth's energy so that she couldn't detach from their passion. She had identified first with one and then the other. But the Moderator was not overwhelmed with emotion, nor was she simply a compromise between the Critic and the Child. She was a separate figure, more objectively analytical than either the Critic or the Child and committed to insuring their survival together. She didn't judge or take sides. She realized who was present and listened to each of them.

Beth's Critic wasn't committed to an ongoing relationship with the Child. That's why the Child looked outside Beth for a man to give her the emotional support she wasn't receiving within. But no man she met was ever committed to an ongoing relationship with the Child, either.

Relationships show you which subpersonalities inside of you need attention. Whatever causes you difficulties in interpersonal relationships reflects an inner relationship that isn't working well. If you are not feeling listened to by your lover, a prominent subpersonality isn't listening to your Child.

There was no way Beth could share a gentle, caring relationship with another human being until that relationship inside her was gentle and caring.

After a year alone, Beth said that she was glad that she had had the relationship with Sam because it brought up her hidden wounds. In therapy she had learned to allow her softer, feeling side to emerge. By surrendering to her feelings, she trusted life and allowed it to guide her to healing.

Men had treated Beth the way her Critic treated the Child. But when her unconscious dynamics changed – when the Critic was no longer hurting the Child and the Child was no longer defending herself – Beth's experience with men changed, too. After a second year alone, Beth wrote to me announcing her engagement. When she didn't need a man to "make her life OK," when she was comfortable with her internal interactions, her unconscious drew a caring man to her. The more experience she had receiving gentleness from a subpersonality within her, the more certain it became that she would receive gentleness from outside her.

Relationships with friends, a lover, or a mate are not mysterious, unknowable affairs. Love is not blind. There is reason and pattern to our experience. We do what we must, acting out what our subpersonalities are doing inside us. The path to harmonious relationships lies within us.

If you are involved in a conflictual relationship, look for projections of a subpersonality in you of whom you're not aware. If a mate is unresponsive, who in you doesn't respond to your Child's needs? If a friend is controlling, what part of you wants to limit your Child's feelings? If a lover is embarrassing to you in public, what subpersonality in you is immature?

Remember, it is no fair saying, "If only s/he were different, then I'd be satisfied." S/he is the way s/he is so that you can see yourself in his/her mirror and take responsibility for your own inner world. If there are changes to be made, they need to happen inside you. The people around you aren't the cause of the problems in your life; they're just a reflection. Look at them and then look inside yourself.

EXERCISE

Before you start this exercise have a pencil and paper ready. You'll want to make notes while you're receiving your imagery so as not to forget it.

Spend several minutes doing the Relaxation exercise on page 9.

Let an image of the two parts of you who conflict about relationships appear. One will be an "anti-relationship" subpersonality and one will be "pro-relationship". Don't think about these parts – just invite them to come and wait until you have a sense of who they are. They may take any form – human figures, animals, inanimate objects. Just watch whatever comes to you. (Pause) Ask it to tell you its three highest values. Listen. (Pause) Without interrupting your meditative state, gently write what you heard and return to your imagery.

Ask the imagery figure what its goals and desires are. (Pause) Listen carefully and write what you hear. Ask this figure how its values and goals affect its relationships. (Pause) Write the answer. Ask it to finish the following sentences and write each response. "I need . . ."

"I want . . ." "I can't stand. . ." Thank that figure for speaking with you.

Now move on to the second figure. Notice the characteristics of this figure. Ask it what its three highest values are. (Pause) Then write what you hear. And ask about its goals and desires. (Pause) And then write. Ask this figure how its values and goals affect its relationships. Listen carefully and write what you hear. (Pause) Ask it to finish the following sentences and write the responses:

"I need . . ."

"I want . . . "

"I can't stand . . ."

Thank this figure for speaking with you.

Have the two figures look at each other. Have one figure describe how it feels when it relates to the other. (Pause) Now give the second figure an opportunity to express its feelings. (Pause) Let them dialogue and write what you hear. Have them each express their frustrations and needs. Allow them to continue interacting as long as they wish. Just watch and listen. (Pause)

Thank them and tell them you will be back to talk with them later. Allow your imagery to fade. Write everything you heard.

REFLECTIONS

Who are your most active subpersonalities in terms of relationships? How do they interact?

How do they handle needs for love and connectedness?

What does your Critic or any similar subpersonality say to you? How does your Child respond to your Critic?

What happens when your Child meets a projection of your Critic in another person?

Chapter 7

HEALING ADDICTION

Even people who don't appear to be Good People are being good in their own minds. Have you ever met a Bitch or a Bastard? Why do you think s/he has given so much energy to that one subpersonality and has hidden the gentle and sensitive Child? Somehow in their lives it's been safer to do that. Being good for them is being tough.

All of us have every kind of subpersonality inside of us. Usually we think of Good People as having developed the "nice" subpersonalities but some Good People develop a different sort of mask. The Bitch or the Con Man or the Jerk predominates and hides the Hurting Child. The purpose of any kind of mask is to shield the inner vulnerability. This can be done by identifying with the Always Available Helper as well as by acting out the Cantankerous Curmudgeon. Whatever subpersonality limited our vulnerability while we were children is strengthened during our growing up years as we rely on it more frequently.

* * * *

Nancy and Jeff sought marital counseling for escalating conflicts. They had been married for three years. Nancy was thirty and Jeff thirty-six.

At our first session Jeff's attire and manner were casual. There was a boyish quality to him that seemed to say that life was to be enjoyed and he knew how to do it. I suspected that many women had found him appealing. When he related his history, he described relationships and affairs before his marriage, confirming my suspicion.

Nancy, tall and slender, was more serious. Her brown eyes narrowed and she looked away as she discussed her concerns. She tried to describe precisely their disagreements and her feelings, but often expressed the dynamics of the relationship in abstract terms. I could tell that she had thought about the marriage problems and had tried to understand them. I guessed that it was at her initiative that they were here. She said:

> He is more likely to wait for me to suggest an activity and to want to be around me. He doesn't want to talk with me about my feelings, but just to have me in the yard working near him. He holds me at arm's length – he won't let go of me and he won't bend his arm so I can move closer. He likes to be sure I'm around, but not too close.

She reported that their communication was unsatisfying for her, that she felt like there was a part of Jeff she "just couldn't reach." When they were dating she felt "swept off her feet by his grand gestures" – a dozen white roses delivered to the office on her birthday, romantic champagne sails at dusk, and beautiful personalized jewelry. He couldn't do enough for her. After their marriage, and increasingly as time passed, she described Jeff as "distant". He was frequently tired or preoccupied when she wanted to talk with him and he never initiated any meaningful conversation. She had suggested therapy previously but he had refused.

Now, he wanted them to have a child. Nancy would not agree to take this step with him unless they received help for what she termed their "lack of intimacy." Because he wanted a family, he agreed to join her in therapy at this time. As he later said, he had to indulge this want of hers in order to get what he wanted. He expected therapy would be brief; he didn't think it would involve a deep commitment.

The three of us met together for three months. Our sessions focused on conflict resolution and improved communication between them. We distinguished between feeling statements ("I feel scared when you walk out the door after a disagreement") and parental control statements ("You shouldn't be talking with him; it's wrong").

Instead of their conflicts diminishing, they increased. Their fights became more frequent and, on Jeff's part, more heated. In addition to fighting with Nancy, Jeff became increasingly hostile to me. He misinterpreted my remarks to him and accused me of being insensitive to his needs. He perceived me as "taking Nancy's position." He refused to talk from his feelings, preferring instead to make "head" statements – "You should. . . That's not realistic. . . We have different philosophies. . ."

Nancy was familiar with these statements. Characteristi-cally, under stress Jeff became more "intellectual," saying what should be, or telling her what was correct to do – usually what he wanted and she didn't. She had repeatedly run into this invisible but totally effective barricade preventing contact between them.

When she observed the same pattern occurring between Jeff and me, she viewed it more objectively and dispassionately. As the three of us talked and Nancy observed Jeff's behavior, it became clear that Jeff didn't want to be open with me or with her and that no one could force him to.

Over the past few years when they reached a point where discussion broke down and no compromise seemed possible, Nancy had thought, "If I give in on this point, he'll appreciate me more and want to be closer." But the more she capitulated, the more demanding Jeff had become. Instead of growing closer, they had become polarized.

As she watched Jeff resist a trusting relationship with me, Nancy saw that the difficulties she had tried to avoid in their relationship were out of her control. She stated,

I am unwilling to compromise my integrity by having Jeff tell me whom I can befriend. I've given up a lot already, but I'm afraid I'll lose myself if I don't remember, and hold onto, what's important to me.

By acknowledging that she wasn't responsible for Jeff's peace of mind or for the harmony in their relationship, Nancy let go of the burden she had unconsciously assumed. Without awareness, she had believed that the outcome of this relationship was up to her. When she saw Jeff interact with me the same way he had interacted with her, she saw that his behavior was totally separate from her and totally his choice. She could "work on the relationship," but in the end she couldn't make him happy. He was responsible for his own happiness.

As Nancy detached from their conflicts, Jeff directed his attention and growing anger towards me. In his mind, I became responsible for their increased emotional distance and for his frustration at not being able to influence Nancy.

After several weeks in which Nancy practiced detachment and Jeff grew more attacking, Nancy decided to separate from him. He had become verbally abusive and she was unwilling to participate in that kind of interaction. She moved out of the area and refused to have contact with him.

Immediately after Nancy's departure, Jeff was furious and punishing towards everyone, but also frantic in his aloneness. He had maintained lots of acquaintances before their marriage but had gradually lost touch with most of his former pals. When Nancy moved away, he terminated our sessions. In his mind I was the cause of their rift and, therefore, an adversary.

Shortly after Nancy's departure, Jeff told me later, he resumed an old pattern of drug abuse. At work his attendance was irregular and his performance unpredictable. He was given an ultimatum by his superiors – either enter a drug rehabilitation program or be fired. He had lost his wife and most of his friends. He couldn't tolerate the thought of losing his job but still he wouldn't commit himself to a rehab center. He was not convinced that he had any problems or that he needed to look within himself. He was still content with criticizing others and blaming them for his losses.

One day after smoking marijuana during his lunch break, he was confronted by his boss who gave him the choice of either entering a drug rehab program that afternoon or leaving work permanently with no hope of being rehired.

In his panic, Jeff agreed to enter the rehab program. He packed a few clothes, drove there, and was introduced to their program. He later wrote about those first days:

> When I saw the doors of the Center, I freaked. If I go in there I won't ever come out, I thought, and in a way I was right. I didn't know then how much of myself I would have to face.

I looked at those doors for a long time. I was just standing there and wondering what I was doing when a young man came out and spoke to me. He told me later that my company had called to alert them I was on my way and he was expecting me. They had also told him that I was pretty recalcitrant. He was kind but clear with me. I had smoked a joint in my car on the way down there. My last one, I thought, until I get out of this place so I might as well enjoy it. He must have known but he didn't say anything. He just took my arm and led me into a small room with a bed and a lamp. I lay on the bed the rest of that evening and spoke to no one, even though I heard people in the hall.

The next day I was scared. I didn't want to be there and I couldn't leave. I didn't want to talk with anyone, but they had compulsory "sharing." A group of druggies sat in a circle and talked about shit from the past and cried. What baloney. When they asked me what my story was I told them I didn't have a story, that there was nothing wrong with me, and that I thought they were all crazy. I didn't want to have anything to do with them and I told them so. Everyone jumped on me. I heard the words "denial" and "asshole." I didn't care what they said. I didn't want to hear it or them. I knew why I was there – because I had to be – and I wasn't going to give anyone anything I didn't have to.

I was able to maintain that attitude for about five days. I avoided people or snapped at them. If anyone tried to be nice to me I pushed him away. I wasn't going to let those jerks do anything to my mind! But, as time passed, I had a harder time staying cool and in control. I needed my "fix." I found myself in a totally new world – no drugs, no job, no buddies, no way of escape.

After hating everyone and everything I became frantic. How was I going to last a whole month? I knew I couldn't just walk out but I didn't think I could stay there, either.

I was right. I couldn't have stayed there and stayed the way I was. They wouldn't accept the wall I had built around myself. Every morning at sharing time someone would attack me, trying to pick away at the wall. And they were a sharp group. They knew all the games. They had been around the block more times than I had so I couldn't fool any one of them.

When I didn't want to participate and said I felt sick, they told me to get off it. No excuse worked with them. I couldn't intimidate them, either. I had always been able to scare off anyone else who got too close to me by growling, but these folks just laughed at me and growled back even louder. Were they tough!

I didn't know what to do. What could I do? I had run all my lines and played all the games I knew and nobody bought any of it. A few days passed. I thought I had caught on to the game all of them played and I faked it. I would say something about a feeling or my childhood and then sit back and think I would be ignored for the rest of the session, but I couldn't even get away with that.

They called me on everything I said and told me I wasn't being honest. I kept getting slammed every sharing session we had. They accused me of "stonewalling". I had heard that word before from Nancy but I had never really listened. I didn't have to. I just tuned her out. Here, I couldn't escape. These guys had me on the hook and wouldn't let go.

One day, they pushed me so hard that I exploded. I yelled at all of them for several minutes and called them every name I had ever heard. While I was raving at them something snapped inside me and I started crying! I was so damned embarrassed but I couldn't stop. The sobs kept coming from someplace deep in my gut and no matter what my head said they just kept coming. I must have bawled there on the floor for twenty minutes. I had never done anything like that. I had absolutely no control. I couldn't stop crying and I couldn't talk. So I just bawled and moaned and screamed in pain and during that time I forgot who I was and where I was. I saw nobody and I heard nothing.

For those twenty minutes I was somewhere else. I went crazy. I didn't think in words or understand what was happening. I was overcome with an unspeakable agony. I had never felt anything like it. It reached way down into my toes and pulled every part of my insides out with it. I thought I had vomited, but it wasn't physical, just loads of hurt and anger and frustration pouring out of me.

When it all stopped, I was holding my knees and rocking with my head in my arms. I was exhausted. I felt like I had been run over by a train that had backed up and run over me again. I couldn't move. I didn't see them, but I became aware that everyone in that group was on the floor with me. When I was calm each one hugged me and spoke to me. I went limp. I couldn't fight them but I didn't hate them. I just wanted to sleep.

When I got to bed I slept for fourteen hours. But instead of feeling stronger when I got up he next day, I felt totally raw. Like someone had scraped away my skin. It hurt to breathe. For the first time I didn't dread the sharing group. Of course, everyone wanted to hear from me first. When I opened my mouth, however, no words would come. Instead I started to cry again! It wasn't the ferocious, violent, gut-wrenching agony from the previous day but deep moans. I went to some part inside of me where I hadn't ever been before. It gave out with these long, deep moans that sounded like a dying animal. It was the strangest experience, almost like I was watching some cord being drawn out of me. It kept coming and coming and I kept moaning. Finally, I only cried. So, I didn't get much talking done that day, either.

Every day that week in group someone said something which got to me. I cried every time! I didn't know I could do that. I felt foolish and a little afraid of what was going to come out of me next, but I was amazed at the same time. Something was happening that I didn't understand. The only experiences I'd had which had been in any way similar to this were when I was doing drugs in school. For a few hours I would be in a different world.

All the rules had changed; nothing happened in the same way as when I was straight. In school, when I tripped with my friends, it was fun – going to Oz for a day. We did it enough that I knew how to get through it. I'd sit back and watch the show.

But this new show without drugs was more intense than anything I'd done before. I was scared. SCARED! I hated these feelings but that didn't even matter. I wasn't the director. I didn't know what was happening and I couldn't stop it. Every time I walked into that group room the strangest things would unfold. I'd walk in as a man and within minutes I'd turn into this sniveling, snot-nosed, whimpering baby. And I couldn't do anything about it. If it hadn't been for the support of the group and the reassurance of Al, our counselor, I would have headed for the hills. This was too bizarre!

That craziness went on for two weeks. No one reminded me of what a jerk I had been or said anything cruel, like "Who's crazy now?" I deserved it but they were right there for me when I needed them. Sure, I still felt lousy and wanted to escape, but I couldn't. My surroundings were safe and unchanging. My insides were nuts!

When I thought I couldn't make it or feel one more damned thing I would talk with Al alone. He had been through all of this himself. He told me about his time on the streets as a junkie for fifteen years before he cleaned up. He really understood what hell I was in. He wasn't a nice clean therapist in a spiffy office with years of school and diplomas on every wall. The man had stolen and lied and slept in doorways and double-crossed every friend he ever had. And finally he made it. I don't know if I could have made it without him or those guys of the safety of those walls in the rehab center.

Nancy had been an angel to me. I see that now, but I hated myself so much I couldn't stand to have her love me. So I just kept hurting her. I really drove her away. I didn't want anything good or beautiful around me. I knew I didn't deserve it. Now I see it was the guilt I couldn't stand when she loved me. She was so precious and I made her life miserable.

I see now how many people I've hurt throughout my life. Anyone who was decent to me I thought was a sucker. So I took all I could get away with and then left them in the dust. I didn't care. I just thought about how I could get what I wanted.

Boy, being in that drug treatment center sure gave me a different perspective. I had always been so selfish. I didn't even know the word "responsibility." I was living inside my own little shell and when I was uncomfortable I would push someone around or pop a pill. But there's only so long anyone can get away with that shit. And in that center it was my time to pay my dues. And did I!

I ended up staying two months. I didn't feel ready to leave when my time was up at the end of one. I was still pretty shaky and not at all sure that I could maintain my new found sobriety. I had learned a lot but I didn't know if it had sifted down from my head into my blood. I was afraid of a relapse. Not only with the drugs but into my old way of being oblivious to my feelings.

So, I stayed and talked and hung out with Al and watched the others go through the cleaning up process. When I got out, it wasn't a day for wild celebrating, as I had expected it would be. I was scared in a different way from before. Now I just wanted to watch every step, to catch every thought and feeling, and to not kid myself anymore. When I left, they gave me a list of recovery meetings – all over the county and on every day and night – that I could attend. I needed that. I didn't trust myself on my own. I knew me too well. I had conned everyone else in my life. I could con myself, too.

Several weeks after Jeff left the treatment center, when he was working again, he called me and we began individual sessions. It had been more than six months since I had talked with him last. He didn't seem to have the energy or excitement that was so evident when I had first met him, but his gaze was steady. He was subdued but not calm. He had done some dramatic work at the rehab center but he was very well aware that all the pieces weren't in place inside of him. His attendance at work was perfect, but now he was smoking cigarettes continuously and sleeping poorly. He had lost twenty pounds and didn't look well.

This time therapy focused on his early life experiences and the development of the subpersonalities upon whom he later relied, eventually to his own detriment. Jeff told me stories about comforting his alcoholic mother when she cried. Her feelings scared him and he wanted to protect her from them. After she had slept off her binge she would be hostile and demeaning to him, calling him names and screaming, "Get out of my sight!" His "mushiness" as he termed it – the fear and the wish to help that he had felt when she was incapacitated – was ridiculed when she was sober.

He vacillated between identifying with his Boy Scout and his Delinquent. He described himself as "careful, attentive, and helpful" when he was in the Boy Scout. When still in that mode of being soft and caring, he would encounter his post-binge mother who was then identified with her Bitch. The Bitch berated and ridiculed the Boy Scout (probably out of guilt, he later thought). But as a kid Jeff only knew that he felt stinging hurt from her words. After having been wounded deeply and repeatedly by her cruel words, he learned not to let himself be vulnerable to her abuse. He learned to protect himself by not wanting appreciation. He stopped hoping for support or even for any acknowledgement of his right to be himself.

For many years he had hoped that his own unique qualities would be noticed. Being appreciated only when Mom was drunk and then being deprived of her favor when she no longer needed him was like having the rug pulled out from under him over and over again. It was done so mercilessly and his pain was so great that, finally, he wouldn't even allow himself to enjoy those moments when Mom did allow closeness (when she was drunk). He shut down the tender part of himself. He no longer wanted or needed kindness. He didn't expect it and wasn't open to receiving it. After so many years of disappointment and betrayal, his Delinquent triumphed in the struggle with the Boy Scout.

Jeff described the Delinquent as an insolent, teen-aged boy. The chip on his shoulder neared the proportions of a boulder. The Delinquent swaggered, scoffed, and mocked. He cared about nothing and no one. He was invulnerable to hurt. He couldn't be affected in any way at all. He had learned that pain always followed closeness and he avoided pain by totally avoiding closeness. No person mattered to him. No achievement was important. Nothing was worth risking humiliation for. The Delinquent protected himself absolutely. Nothing and no one would devastate him the way the Boy Scout had been devastated. The Delinquent was self-sufficient behind his walls.

Jeff could flirt with and charm women, but they were only a challenge to him. He seduced them and dropped them. He revelled in his reputation as a "heart-breaker." No woman would ever destroy him. Not again. He toyed with women, honing his acting skills expertly, practicing his role as Flamboyant Seducer.

By definition, that role had a time limit with any one woman, however. After the seduction, his anxiety increased as his acting skills were exhausted. He had no other part of himself he was willing to share. Therefore, he had to bow out of relationships before any feelings could develop on his part.

Jeff wrote in his journal:

I don't know where my heart was during those years. I didn't have any lows. My highs happened when I was acting, and I did get good at that. I was so believable. I could charm the pants off any woman and that's exactly what I wanted to do. The guys at the bar called me The Conqueror. I thought it was a joke. Now I see how really angry I was. I left so many women in tears and I thought I really liked that, but you don't treat people that way and walk away feeling comfortable with yourself. Still it made me feel powerful like nothing else had.

There were so many times in my childhood when I thought I would collapse 'cause I ached so badly. I hated that weakness in myself. When I saw that weakness in women I thought they were stupid and childish. They asked for it. They didn't take care of themselves. I had convinced myself that it was every person for himself and that you couldn't blame anyone if you got hurt.

I always solved my "problems" by running away, although I didn't realize it at the time. I saw my feelings as problems and the source of humiliation. I hated myself when I would feel anything. It seemed that when I cared, I go humiliated, and when I wanted someone to like me, I got criticized.

Who needs it? I stopped wanting and stopped hoping I would receive kindness. I became the toughest Bastard around. That saved me from the roller coaster rides that naive Boy Scout always got himself on. I couldn't be destroyed. I couldn't even be touched. I was so far away from where everyone else was, it was funny. They thought that when they talked to me I really cared about what they were saying. I could fool anyone. Disdain became my primary way of relating. No one saw it until a long time after they knew me, though.

Now I see how I was repeatedly punishing Mom for abandoning me when I depended on her. Over and over again, I would get women to depend on me and then I'd toss them away. I knew how that felt and I wanted someone to pay for my agony. Not only could no woman hurt me, I hurt as many of them as I could. Now I see I was doing it all to strengthen my belief in my ability to stand on my own in the world. When my mother would ignore me when I was so young and I needed her, I thought I would die. When I developed my wall, I thought I could live if no pain intruded from the outside world to again hurt me. Then I truly felt powerful if I could make someone else feel pain while I felt nothing. That was what I saw adults doing when I was a kid so I thought I was being just like them. At last I wasn't that helpless kid anymore. I could play the game.

The drugs helped me hold onto The Conqueror. I tried everything. There wasn't a drug that scared me. My body was invincible. I really thought I had life licked. I was on top of the whole world and no one could push me off. At last I was where I wanted to be all my life. People looked up to me and I looked down on them.

Even in my marriage I kept myself pretty well walled off. I always liked Nancy but I was careful never to let myself love her or need her. The longer we stayed married, though, the more difficult that became. She was such an innocent. She just kept loving me and taking it upon herself to fix any problems we had. I let her take care of everything. Hell, if that's what she wanted, that was OK with me. She started to change, though. I don't know what it was – the women at her work or those self-help books she was always reading – but she slowly started pulling away from me.

I thought it was OK for *me* to act like that, but it was totally *not* OK when I realized that she no longer depended on me. When she started pulling away,

I redoubled my efforts to snow her. She's smart, though. She recognized my game and didn't buy my hype. She didn't get hysterical, either, or complain or cry or get hurt. She kept her cool and just continued to move away from me.

That drove me crazy. I wasn't the one in control any longer. It had always been my role to do the leaving. I didn't want to be the one who was left. But that's just what was happening and I couldn't prevent it. She didn't fall for my gifts or my lines. So all that garbage I had buried finally surfaced. I attacked her. I said awful things to her and tried to get her to come back to me that way. She used to love a challenge, but now it didn't even tempt her. But then I was inspired! I told her I wanted a child. I knew she wanted one even though she had never said too much about it. This was something she would respond to.

I really did get her attention with that one, too. I thought having a child could help us ignore all the other stuff – what she called communication problems – but she wasn't thrown off the track for more than a day. Instead of smoothing over our problems, they became huge. Now she picked up on every little tiny thing I said and did and she wanted to know what it meant. Why was I doing that? What relation to my past did it have? Cripes! It drove me mad. I totally lost my cool then. She got every bit of leftover resentment and frustration I could find. I dumped it all on her. And when she backed off I got even crazier!

I drove her to move out when that was what I most wanted to avoid. Every ploy I could think of to hold onto her backfired and when she was gone I was lonelier than I had ever felt in my life. What a loser I was then. But no one saw it or so I thought. I told the guys at work I had asked her to leave. I acted like I was glad she was gone. Probably they all saw through me. Hell,

I was just holding on by my fingertips. I needed drugs then. There was nothing else to depend on.

When my boss got in my face at work, I could tell he knew. I had no more excuses, no escape. Where could I go? What could

I say? I had to go to the rehab center but only 'cause all the other doors had closed. I had run out of tricks.

Jeff was unusually clear – in both his eyes and his thoughts. He knew that he had removed a lot of the coverings – the drug abuse, the anger, the violent outbursts – but he also knew he wasn't living fully, either. Releasing the symptoms had only focused the internal pain. Now, neither the Delinquent nor the Boy Scout prevailed. He had no roles to hide behind and without the roles he couldn't hide his inner emptiness. Now he was painfully aware of the void inside him. He felt no inner support structure, no frame upon which to hang a personality.

We spent part of each therapy session in visualization. By doing that, Jeff had an opportunity to release his identification with his ego roles and to contact an innate wisdom within him. He needed the calm and the perspective which came when he closed his eyes and got away from his conscious mind. Through visualizing, Jeff learned to look at how he perceived and experienced himself and the world instead of identifying with his perceptions. He noticed how he saw instead of concentrating on what he saw. This awareness became our focus.

Through paying attention to his gaping inner wound, Jeff acknowledged his unmet need for love, nurturing, and consistent support. His Needy Child was very much in evidence when the drugs, the anger, and the withdrawal fell away. In his visualizations, Jeff encountered his Child with its intense pain. He felt the devastation but he also saw it from a higher perspective. In addition to being the Child, he was also the Observer of the Child.

Jeff described his experiences visualizing from the perspective of a cloud:

> I gradually loosen my hold on my normal way of seeing. I go to another place – usually on my cloud – and I observe from there. I'm safe and I don't have to protect myself from attack. No one else is a threat to me when I'm on my cloud.

No one has ever really been an enemy or the cause of my problems. I could only see that when I got to the cloud. I fought with anyone else to avoid confronting myself. When I do look inside and I face my Needy Child, my heart breaks. I can't seem to comfort him enough to relieve his never ending pain. He's in agony and I can't do a thing about it. It scares me.

By moving to the cloud Jeff was outside the Child so that he didn't drown in the Child's emotion. He also could see the Child's boundaries from that perspective; thus, he knew the Child's feelings *did* end at a certain line. The need and the pain weren't limitless. He could choose when and how long he wanted to be with the Child, but he had to spend some time with him every day. From the cloud he could do it. When he was on the cloud Jeff was calm and anchored, touched by the Child's pain but not overwhelmed by it.

After months of experiencing peace on the cloud, observing the Child, and feeling as much of the Child's pain as he could, Jeff felt stronger. He wasn't afraid of his inner world and didn't feel compelled to avoid it. The cloud was always present inside and Jeff could consciously go to it when he chose. He did often and began to identify with the peace and the feeling of being centered that it offered. He once stated that he was as addicted to the cloud as he had been to drugs or to anger. He had found an inner source of support for his dependency that allowed him to be flexible. He could move into and out of his feelings easily.

More and more frequently, Jeff spoke with a new voice. It was slower and slightly deeper. He paused before he spoke; he was checking inside to hear the words before he verbalized them. Jeff named his new prominent inner subpersonality the Gentle Father. He described what Gentle Father qualities meant to him:

My mother was so easy to see that I thought she was my only significant early relationship. A shame. Because there was *no way* I wanted to be like her. But I did have another parent. How could I ignore him? (Probably because he ignored me.)

Anyway, my corollary inner Father also seemed absent. I think of assertiveness, firmness, clarity, and focus as being father qualities. All of those characteristics combine to make strength. Strength comes from inside and it's flexible. My walls used to seem strong to me but they were just rigid. Strength is gentle. As I remove the walls that isolate my Needy Child, the gentle strength slowly emerges. I hear the strength in the new voice that comes out of me sometimes. He's my ideal father. The first time around (in my real life), I didn't really experience having a Father, but that wasn't my last chance. Why do we always think that what exists physically is all there ever is?

Now I have a relationship with my inner Gentle Father. He's highly responsible in several ways. He's not interested in how much he can get away with. He doesn't think of himself as a Loser who has to connive in order to get what he needs. He truly is an adult. When he has commitments to meet, he meets them. They don't scare him.

The Delinquent couldn't stand the restrictions he thought commitments imposed on him. Therefore, he always had to be devising some undercover deal in his mind. He didn't play fair with anyone; he always had a card he didn't show. I've always really known that I've acted like a jerk. I was playing a game with the whole world and guess who the chump turned out to be?

The Gentle Father in me insists that I be honest – with everyone else but basically with myself. He demands that I recognize other people's feelings and respect them. No more games. That's essentially the message he gives me. No more screwing around. No more living as if what counts comes "later." THIS IS IT. My life is now. He's absolutely committed to being decent – in business and with friends.

Starting with knowing the group in the rehab center and continuing with the people at my meetings, I'm understanding what friendship is. Friends are people you don't have to scam. I can be honest and they still want me around. They don't judge me or compare me or criticize me. They listen to me and want me to listen to them. It's a completely different way of relating from anything

I've ever experienced before. I have nothing to gain or lose from them. Nothing material, just the richness of life and being known and being touched.

Now I know what Nancy meant when she said I was untouchable. I was without my Gentle Father. I couldn't trust anyone else or myself. I didn't know myself. I wasn't sure I could make it on my own. I was so damned scared! I thought I was protecting myself from being hurt but I was just holding all my old hurts inside. I kept them alive instead of feeling them and letting them go. I couldn't let in anyone who would love me. I guess I knew that feeling anything new would bring up all those old hurts. I didn't want to do that no matter what the cost!

I only paid that cost at the rehab center when I had enough strong support around me that the world wouldn't fall apart even if I did. So I fell apart but, hell, that was the best place I could have done it! Al and the group understood me and didn't let me get away with my shit. Al was the first strong Gentle Father I'd ever known. He really was an honorable man. He looked simple, but he took responsibility for everything he said and did. If I wanted to talk to him he made time for me and he really listened. He heard every word I said, but more importantly, he heard me beneath the words.

He came up against who I really was, and he made me face that person, too. I didn't like what I saw and sometimes he didn't, either, but he always accepted me. Yeah, I was a jerk a lot but he knew that I was more than that, too. Being a jerk was just a stupid cover because I was too scared to be honest. Well, he demanded honesty. He gave me all he had and he didn't let me give any less. He wanted all of me and wouldn't settle for my cover. I couldn't scam him and that saved my life.

Nancy was wonderful but I was killing myself with her. She just wasn't tough enough for me and that's what I needed. Now my Gentle Father is tough with me. Never vicious but always brutally honest. I trust his guidance. With Al as a model for a while and then my sponsor for the meetings, I could find that Gentle Father inside me. Now I talk and listen to him every day. Every day. I don't make a move without consulting him. If I don't follow his guidelines of absolute honesty and complete responsibility, I pay and the price seems to be getting higher. Deception worked OK when I was a kid but the rules changed sometime when I wasn't looking. Now, it's strictly straight and narrow for me.

When one way-of-being stops working for us – and it always does at some point if it's based on fear – we need to switch our allegiance. At that point we allow an Adult to prevail responsibly.

Our childhood basis for living cannot possibly encompass our adult talents and needs. As children we usually have very little inner strength and much dependency. If the adults we depend on have their own quirks and blind spots (and who doesn't?) we adjust. We don't know we're doing this; we just learn to live however we must. Whatever subpersonality helps us to do that is favored.

When we cling to one subpersonality, we ignore others and prevent inner integration and growth. We live incompletely. However, we usually find that life puts an end to that. We're allowed leeway in our early lives but sometime in our thirties or forties our manipulations cease to provide the reward they once did. Parents are no longer around and the world has a way of pointing out our distortions. Our manipulations aren't effective. Everything we "know" becomes useless. We now must release the defenses which have kept us unaware of the deeper parts of ourselves and look at what we've feared.

Life decides for us when our time of reckoning is. Our protestations and arguments are irrelevant. When it's time to face ourselves, it's time. It seldom happens all at once and it never happens without the support we need – outside or inside.

No one has ever died from feeling repressed pain. And after we've felt it, we integrate the parts of ourselves we had cut off. We thought we couldn't survive with them during the first part of lives; now we can't survive wholly without them. The authenticity which follows from our openness to ourselves allows us to live fully and richly. Without our fears or hurts limiting us, we can allow life to guide us through providing us with the experiences we need. Being fully and flexibly human is the goal. Life will give us the experiences we need; we just have to recognize and accept them.

Which subpersonality did you rely on most when you were young? How did it help you? What do you say when you are identified with that part of you?

Which subpersonalities did you hide when you were young? Do you hide your Needy Child now? How?

Which subpersonalities do you currently identify with and which do you project onto others?

Think of one relationship you have and describe your interactions in terms of each person's subpersonalities. Each of you may identify with several subpersonalities at different times in your interactions. What do you notice?

Who is a mature subpersonality in you with whom you need to stay in touch? What does that subpersonality tell you?

EXERCISE

Do the relaxation exercise on page 9.

Let an image come to you. In your image two of your subpersonalities are struggling. It may be a conflict you have had for years or it may be a recent choice that's hard to make. Just watch these two. (Pause) Who are the two subpersonalities? (Pause) Notice the characteristics of their interaction. (Pause) What does each say and do? (Pause)

Allow the interaction to continue and notice that your soul ascends out of the scene to a cloud directly above these two figures. (Pause) From that cloud, look at whatever you see around you. What do you notice? (Pause) Breathe and experience being on that cloud. (Pause)

Remaining on the cloud, look down on the two subpersonality figures below you. (Pause) Notice each figure from the cloud perspective. (Pause) What do you notice about their interaction from this perspective that you couldn't see from below? (Pause)

Descend directly from the cloud into the scene with the two figures. (Pause) You have brought with you your experience from the cloud. Notice what happens in the scene. (Pause) Is there a shift or change? (Pause) If some kind of resolution occurs, notice how it happens. (Pause)

REFLECTIONS

Who were the two interacting subpersonality figures? What was their interaction about?

How did it feel being on the cloud?

What did you see when you looked around you?

How did these two figures look from the cloud perspective?

Did you notice anything from the cloud that you hadn't seen before? After your soul descended from the cloud, what happened?

Chapter 8

LISTENING TO THE BODY

Ann was a nurse with dark blond hair and lively brown eyes. She bounced rather than walked and bubbled rather than spoke. Her small body seemed to percolate. In her late twenties, Ann was frequently mistaken for eighteen. She lived by her feelings and often felt caught in a whirlwind. However, her buoyancy masked an underlying constriction and depression.

When she began therapy, Ann had difficulty articulating her goals. She was restless and dissatisfied but could not precisely identify a problem. Life just wasn't turning out the way she had always expected it would. She was doing the same things she saw her friends doing, but she felt like she was "only going through the motions." Nothing had much meaning to her and the anchor of traditional values seemed to weigh her down rather than ground her. "I'm living in ways I was taught to, but I don't really feel like I'm living at all." Her appearance was not an accurate indicator of her feelings.

Psychological thinking was natural for Ann. She could discuss her feelings and wants, but only to a point. Before she could experience a peaking of emotion and a consequent resolution, something in her tightened and the feeling vanished. She was left numb, feeling less alive. Then her efforts at vivacity were increased in a desperate fight against the engulfing deadness. She felt like she was "drowning in quicksand" and struggling for breath. But, as in quicksand, the struggle didn't resolve her frustrations; it only led her to sink deeper, to feel more cut off from herself and everyone else, and to try anxiously to force the joie de vivre she couldn't seem to feel naturally.

Ann's blanketing numbness left her without words to speak clearly about the details of her inner experience but, being extroverted, Ann was aware of how others responded to her. She preferred to focus on her relationships. An imbalance inside of her was obvious, but we approached her inner world through the outer. After all, inner or outer – both lead us to the same conflicts.

Ann had lots of dates but was dissatisfied with the relationships after a few weeks. She understood that the men she met reflected parts of herself to her and she didn't like what she saw.

She noticed several patterns in her relationships. One type of man she was attracted to was young and exciting. He wasn't committed to a career or a mortgage. He was seductive but inconsistent. These men would take her dancing or to parties with their friends. They were great fun. For two or three weeks. But when Ann wanted to know them better, to see deeper than the "good time" facade, they disappeared. What could these men be showing me about myself? Ann wondered.

In several imagery sessions we invited the young, inconsistent subpersonality in Ann to speak to us. We closed our eyes and breathed for a few moments. An image appeared to Ann of a teenage girl. She reported the following interaction:

Observer: Please tell me about yourself.

Teenager: I am you – your feelings and your wants. I can get men to love me. I want attention and so I've learned that the way to get attention is by listening, by getting men to talk about themselves and by showing only my sweet side.

Observer: Yes, I recognize you. You take over when there's fear and the Adult doesn't know what to do.

Teenager: I can manage to get through any situation by flattering people. I know what they want to hear and I tell them.

Observer: Something about that sounds uncomfortable.

Teenager: I'm just doing what will make people love me.
Observer: Does everyone love you when you do your "act"?

Teenager: Not everyone. With women, especially older women, it works well. With young men it works well enough for them to love me for an evening or a week. We go to bed but they don't call back.

Observer: That must feel terrible.

Teenager: Yes. (crying softly) I don't know how to make anyone love me for a long time.

Observer: You can't force love to happen, can you?

Teenager: No, and it scares me that I will always be alone. No one stays around. What's wrong? What should I do differently?

Observer: You're such a confused, hurt kid. Let me be with you. I may not have any solutions for you but at least you don't have to do your act with me.

Ann realized that her Teenager was a Child with a teenager's appearance, doing adult things. The Child wanted to be loved and the Teenager thought of teenage ways of getting love. Love became a matter of manipulation, giving people what they wanted in hopes that they would then depend on her so much they wouldn't leave her. (Ann made the connection between this way of thinking and her choice of nursing as a career. How could a dependency relationship be acted out more completely than with people who needed her for their physical survival?)

Obviously, neither Ann's Child nor her Teenager had a sense of receiving love freely given. She couldn't accept the fact that some people wouldn't love her. The Teenager thought that if someone didn't love her, it was her fault and she could change. She didn't want to relinquish her belief that there was a simple and rational logic to life – that what happened to her was a consequence of how hard she tried to be good. Circumstances had never proved this belief to be true, but she continued to try to make it true.

Ann understood that she was holding onto a childhood notion in her Teenager subpersonality. The Child/Teenager was relating to everyone she met as though they were parents to be pleased. And she continued to employ the methods which had pleased her parents – being focused on their needs and denying her own. That pleasing act had worked with her parents, but trying to get love from everyone one else that way hadn't given her a stable, long-lasting sense of her own value and worth. She did receive approval for her act sometimes from some people, but this merely perpetuated an unsatisfying pattern. In fact, this way of manipulating for love reinforced her belief that, as a person, she wasn't valuable. Her only worth came from what she could do for another. And so the cycle continued.

Another type of man Ann unconsciously attracted to her was initially solicitous. Then, after she was interested in him, he became distracted and withdrawn. He would forget dates or be an hour late. She felt like she had been picked up and dropped with no warning. She didn't understand what was going on in these men's minds; she just kept waiting for them. When they did appear she was pleasant and didn't mention her disappointment.

With our eyes closed we breathed and invited anyone inside to speak to us about this uncomfortable pattern. After a few minutes Ann reported that she felt anger. Her Adult was impatient with her Child for tolerating such poor treatment. The Child seemed to be so needy!

She was always making herself available to people – especially irresponsible men – and was always being abandoned in the end. Ann heard them talk:

Adult: How can you allow yourself to be treated so inconsiderately? It infuriates me to see how these men treat you and how you just accept it.

Child: What else can I do?

Adult: Yell, scream, kick them in the knee. Do something!

Child: (Whimpering) I can't. I just can't. I can't take care of myself. I need someone to take care of me. That's what I always hope a man will do for me.

Adult: They never do, though, do they? So why do you still hope? Are you stupid?

Child: (Now crying) I guess I am. Maybe the next man, if there is one, will love me.

Adult: Let's not talk about love. I don't think that's really what's happening here at all. I think it's dependency. You want someone else to take away your scared feelings and make you happy.

Child: (Brightening) Sounds good to me!

Adult: Well, it won't happen. Your feelings are your life. You have to love them and hold them and accept them.

Child: I'm too little.

Adult: OK, you exasperate me but I will have to care as much about you as I'm asking you to care about yourself. I'll protect and guide you. I can do a better job of loving you than any man can, anyway.

Child: (Warily) What will you do for me?

Adult: I can be consistent and I'll always be sensitive to your feelings.

Child: You haven't been around for me before. Why will you be available now?

Adult: Because you're getting into painful situations using no judgment with men who don't treat you decently. I can't stand the pain.

Child: You haven't treated me any differently from the way these men do. You expect me to be nice. You'd rather be with anyone other than me.

Adult: I know I've treated you insensitively in the past. I'm sorry. What I would like to do in the present and the future is to listen to your wants, but I want to be the one making the relationships in the world. You won't have to go to anyone else; I will take care of you. I can't trust that you will handle yourself appropriately with others so let me be in charge of relationships.

Child: Well, if you are always available to me . . . But, wait, what about when I want to be held?

Adult: I'll hold you. I'll listen to you. I'll let you cry or be angry.

Child: It's not the same.

Adult: Right! I don't want our relationship to be the same a the awful relationships you've been getting into. I want it to work out better. I realize that it's been my disregard for your feelings that has led you to approach other people to get what you wanted. It has never worked out so I will sincerely commit to you that I want a relationship to work out between us.

Child: Well, that's a commitment I've never heard from a man.

Adult: See? Already you're seeing how much I care.

Ann's Child, with her need for love, had finally made contact with her Adult. Previously, her Adult had ignored the Child. When the Child wanted attention she was on her own, devising her Child means to get it from others. The Adult hadn't contributed her Adult judgment. The two subpersonalities had always worked alone. This was the first conversation in which the Adult had acknowledged the Child's wants and taken them seriously. Now the Adult had promised to contribute her skills, to cooperate with the Child in meeting her needs rather than ignoring her. As long as the Adult ignored her, the Child was certain to be frustrated.

For all of us, the Child tells us our wants and needs but the Adult tells us how to meet our needs successfully. So, cooperation between the two is necessary if the Child is to be happy and the Adult satisfied.

In her commitment to focus upon the relationships among her subpersonalities, Ann decided to stop dating for awhile. She had gathered information about her internal relationships by looking at her relationships with others and was now ready to apply what she had learned to the ongoing process within her. She had developed a rhythm – first focusing on the outside relationships to gather data and then focusing inside to use the data to alter her own dynamics.

From her subpersonality conversations, Ann realized that her Adult must listen to her Needy Child and develop a strong relationship with her. That Child had never experienced a consistent loving relationship that wasn't built on service or manipulation. So her Adult decided to show her what that would be like. The Adult treated the Child with the same genuine kindness and caring that

Ann gave to her patients. She checked in with the Child to ask what she wanted each day. Anytime Ann felt off-center, she knew the Child needed to speak with the Adult. She began to recognize the cues that her Child gave when she wanted attention; when Ann was restless and couldn't concentrate, her Adult asked her Child what she wanted. When the Child was satisfied she settled down and Ann could continue with her Adult work. Providing anything her Child needed became the Adult's priority.

Ann saw the failure of her Child/Teenager to mature. They were stuck back in a reality which didn't exist any longer. Her parents had both been young professionals during Ann's early childhood. They provided all of the "things" any child could need but didn't stay around long themselves. They were very busy in their careers. From relating to them, Ann learned to be undemanding emotionally. She didn't present them with any needs; they didn't have time for that. If the world (as interpreted by her parents) couldn't handle her needs, she just wouldn't have any.

In this environment, some subpersonalities were encouraged to grow, while others were severely limited. Her self-reliant Little Adult was given prominence, while her dependent Wimp was pushed aside. Her take-charge-of-the-situation Leader received approbation, while her frightened Recluse receded. From the very subtle conditioning of her parents' attention when she was strong and their withdrawal when she was needy, Ann learned the act that would be rewarded and then she continued this conditioning inside herself. She valued some parts of herself and disregarded others. And so, Ann (unconsciously) structured her own inner world in an imbalanced, frustrating, and sabotaging way.

Her inner world belonged to Ann. It was not interpersonal and it was not something that had happened in the past. The relationship between her Adult and her Child was the basis for her experience with other people in the world. And she was totally responsible for the state of affairs within her. Ann wrote about her experience of the reconciliation process between her Adult and her Child in her journal:

> My Adult sits quietly for two or three minutes and breathes and relaxes and forgets about her concerns. When she is genuinely able to be present to the Child, she asks the Child to come sit with her and tell her her feelings. The Child says she is scared. The Adult allows the Child to be afraid and doesn't fight her or try to dissuade her. No matter what the Child feels, it is OK with the Adult. She stays right with the Child and holds her. The Adult accepts the intensity of all of the Child's feelings and lets them be, just as they are.

When the Child has spent her emotion, the Adult uses her discerning mind to hear the beliefs from which those feelings sprang. Fear stems from the belief that "No one will protect me and I may die." Loneliness comes from the belief that "I am an unlovable person if I act just the way I feel." Neediness develops from the belief that, "It's better to take care of others than to want them to take care of me."

Ann listed these unconscious beliefs that she heard the Child communicate: I have no value unless I serve others.

I will be abandoned if I am honest about my feelings and my needs. It's not safe to trust anyone.

I can't have what I want. My needs are insatiable. I am very angry.

Only those people who depend on me will stay with me.

As she went through this process, carefully and precisely elucidating her unconscious beliefs, Ann let them go. She couldn't separate from them until she was aware of what she was holding onto. As they became conscious, her responsibility in maintaining her own reality became clear. She had been unconsciously proving these basic beliefs true over and over and over again.

She validated the belief, "I can't have what I want," by choosing to have relationships with men who couldn't meet her needs. With the belief, "I will be abandoned if I am honest about my feelings," she could recognize that unconsciously she had chosen persons in her life who would certainly abandon her because of who they were, not because of who she was. It only looked like they were reacting to her. Really they were just doing what they do – withdrawal and abandonment.

Through these beliefs, her Child had created understanding and meaning to explain her experience. Whatever she felt and whatever happened to her were filtered through these beliefs. Any experience could be distorted to fit these unconscious "truths." If someone left her, it was because "I have no value." If she were unsatisfied in a relationship, it was because "My needs are insatiable." She always referred back to these unconscious beliefs to explain her disappointments.

Nothing in Ann's life assumed greater importance than the Adult insuring the comfort of the Child. As her Child was happier, she asked for less and contributed to Ann's delight in everyday events. The Child didn't want to be a drain on Ann but when she was scared and needy, she couldn't be anything else. With the Adult's attention she became less needy, appropriately trusting, and generally happier. Instead of being a nuisance to Ann, she offered her a way of looking at the world which was creative and fun – the world became a place to play and expect joyful surprises.

While gaining more perspective on her relationships internally and externally, Ann began to think about the men she met as being projections of her masculine figure inside. The men she encountered must have similar characteristics to her inner Male. The thought made her shudder.

So she knew she must listen to her inner Male. She relaxed, allowing her mind to become blank. She focused on her breath and invited her inner Male to show himself to her. She wrote in her journal:

His name was Ralph. Ugh. I've always disliked that name. He's no pleasant sight, either. He's fat, unclean, and retarded. I disliked him immediately. He knew it and didn't like me for it. So I realized that I would have to spend time with him.

I sat with him at dinner and taught him how to use silverware. He had no table manners so I made some suggestions about keeping his mouth closed and his elbows off the table. He wanted to gulp his food, but I encouraged him to eat slowly and enjoy his dinner. The change in him was surprising. He appreciated the attention and responded to my suggestions. He knew he needed some education in living gracefully and took in everything I said. I felt like I was with a young man who hadn't had any social experience. (I've felt the same way with a couple of my boyfriends!) Ralph was ready to learn and was waiting to be acknowledged.

Next Day

This morning when I was walking, I called to Ralph and asked him to be with me. When he came he was different from last night. He was dark, physically very fit, and proud of his athletic body. As I walked, he sprinted back and forth. This time he was talking to *me*, educating *me* in areas he thought I had neglected. He was very sensual and talked to me about including an appreciation of the sensual in my life – take time to appreciate beauty around me, feel textures, be aware of subtleties. Oh, yes, and he said his name was Mr. Rolf. I thought he could add some nice touches to my life, including some deeper levels of awareness, so I could live more fully. He interested me; I wanted to know him better.

Next Day

Today when we spoke, Ralph/Mr. Rolf had changed again. In fact, he told me his name is Raul. He is Mexican and earthy. He loves women. He spoke to me about sexuality in gentle terms. He seems to understand just how hard that is for me – being present to my feelings at the same time I am present to my body – so he doesn't push me or make fun of me. He did suggest that I try little exercises, like lying on the floor and feeling whatever is going on in my body at the moment. He was careful not to embarrass me or to push me faster than he knew I could go.

He seems to know me precisely and to respect me, but to be very different from me. He owns all of those characteristics I don't consciously acknowledge – my aggression, my anger, my sexuality. He seems foreign yet familiar. I can't predict the way he thinks, but it doesn't surprise me. I understand him, but I haven't had his experiences.

He is much more comfortable with his body and his instincts than I am with mine. Even though I've slept with men, I've done it for their approval, not really out of my body for sensual pleasure or out of my mature feelings of wanting to give love. It was another manipulation, a way of giving a man what I thought he wanted in order to keep him with me.

Raul lives out of his insides. He isn't intellectual, just very grounded. He moves over the earth like a sleek cat. He knows what is real but is unconcerned with ideas. He is sure of himself and the world because he lives out of his physical nature. He can feel and see and he trusts his senses. He knows because he experiences. His body and its experience are his bases for making decisions.

After several weeks Ann noticed that, although she wasn't calling upon a masculine figure as a distinct part of her, her behavior in general was different. Without effort, she was becoming assertive and self-protective. A major shift she noticed was that her body seemed to be pulling her back to her own sexuality. She noticed sexual feelings and, more surprisingly, she found herself willing to stroke her body. She had been raised strictly and had never touched herself, but now her body wanted to be touched. She felt deep flows move within her and she was responsive to her own touch. She wrote in her journal:

Living from within my body means that I am pulled, not pushed. My mind doesn't pressure, cajole or criticize. Rather, I am compelled by some deeper intuition. My image is of a rope coming out of my solar plexus that extends in front of me. I can't see where it is attached on the other end, but it draws me. I allow it to lead me into experiences which turn out to be perfect for me. In little ways, my intuition guides me through my days, gently tugging me to the left or to the right or encouraging me to be still. As I follow its lead, I am given gifts – an unexpected encounter, a beneficial coincidence.

Whatever is pulling me on the long rope has an unerring sense of timing. When I go with it, I experience exactly what I need to, but what my mind with its control cannot predict. I can see now how my mind's control is good for some things – I need it when I'm pressing a straight crease in my slacks or when the accountant wants my tax information – but it can't help me in other ways. It isn't any good at living creatively or at celebrating. That's not its job. I have to listen to my intuition and my body for that.

This rope seems to connect me to a level of life where there's magic – a wonderland where everything is connected and flows together easily. I don't jump out of bed to go exercise but instead rest. I receive a phone call I value but would have missed if I were "being good, doing what I should." There is an underlying order and pattern and flow to everything which I didn't experience when I was busy following my head's commands. It's not my head's fault; I asked it to keep me safe and it did that the only way it could – by using control. But when I don't need safety, I don't need control. Now I need aliveness and connection. That's what I look to my body/feelings/intuition for. I'll give my head a rest. It has worked so hard for me but now I'll let my body pull me. There's no effort to that! It just takes my letting go and being willing to follow. And I am!

Ann became increasingly spontaneous and less "careful." She sought out fun times and people and reduced her working time. She began to see life as an adventure. She felt like she was given gifts and only had to be willing to receive them and experience her own feelings. Her sense of being loved expanded. Not only could she imagine being loved by individuals around her, but also that she had a place in the world, physical and spiritual. She knew in her heart that she was acceptable as a person and that anything she would hear from inside her was acceptable, also.

Ann noticed that her subpersonalities changed over time and that some new ones appeared. She said that it reflected her maturing process. She realized that she had sacrificed true maturity in order to play roles she thought would earn approval. She developed a new definition of maturity – knowing and accepting her inner world with all of it subpersonalities.

EXERCISE

Spend several minutes doing the Relaxation exercise on page 9.

Imagine yourself entering a room in which there are several figures seated at a table and one empty chair. Walk over and sit in the empty chair. (Pause) Notice the table. What is its shape? Of what is it made? (Pause)

Notice how many figures are seated at the table. (Pause) Are they human, animal, plant, mineral, or something else? (Pause) Turn and look at the figure on your left. (Pause) Notice that figure's gender, body posture, facial expression, and breathing. (Pause) The figure has a name tag on his/her left shoulder stating the name or label for the subpersonality s/he represents. What is on the name tag? (Pause) Ask that figure to speak to you describing what s/he does for you. (Pause) Have him/her tell you about a time in your life when she was prominent, controlling the action in your life. Listen. (Pause)

When s/he is finished, focus upon the figure to his/her left. Again notice the gender, body posture, facial expression, and breathing. (Pause) Read that figure's name tag. (Pause) Have that figure tell you what s/he does for you and when s/he was prominent in your life. Listen. (Pause)

When that figure is finished, continue attending to each figure around the table, repeating the process. (Pause) (Even if the figures are people you know, they still represent some part of you. If you are not sure which part, ask them. If you are still confused, let three adjectives come to mind describing the figure. These adjectives describe the part of you that figure represents.)

After each figure has spoken, suggest that they discuss some issue of current concern to you. Notice who starts the discussion. (Pause) Who dominates the discussion? (Pause) Who is quiet? (Pause) Which two figures interact most?

(Pause) Which are adversaries? (Pause) Which are allies? (Pause) Is any one a leader? (Pause) Watch and listen. Notice how the conversation progresses.

Now you see another subpersonality on the ceiling. That figure has always been there but you haven't noticed him/her before. S/he has been watching everything that has transpired. S/he understands each figure at the table well. As they become quiet, s/he speaks to each figure in turn. S/he knows precisely what message each one needs to receive. Listen to what she tells each figure. (Pause) After s/he has given each figure a message, the subpersonality on the ceiling has a message for you. Listen. (Pause) What are you told? (Pause)

Notice how the different figures interact after they have received their messages. (Pause) Is there a resolution or a conclusion to the discussion?

Now write.

Describe your imagery. What were the details of the room and the table? Describe each figure with its name tag and what each one said.

Describe the discussion among them. What was the topic? What were the positions the different figures took?

Who dominated and who was quiet?

Which two interacted the most and what was the nature of their interaction?

Each of the figures represents a subpersonality. What part does each subpersonality play in your life?

What part of you is the subpersonality on the ceiling?

What were the messages that the ceiling figure gave to each subpersonality and to you?

REFLECTIONS

What have you done in your life when you wanted approval? Which subpersonality was motivating you?

Who is the most sexual subpersonality in you? Does s/he have an adversary? Who?

Which of your subpersonalities is projected onto your partner or someone else?

Which of your subpersonalities has been relegated to your unconscious (pushed away from you because you didn't want to see it)?

Have you been ignoring some parts of you in order to act "mature"?

Chapter 9

LISTENING TO SPIRIT

Sally is a Catholic sister. She entered the convent after high school when she was seventeen. Now at thirty-four, she has chronic mononucleosis, long lasting colds, and migraines. Sally looks ten years older than she is, due to the dark circles around her eyes and her very thin body. In addition to the sense of exhaustion that hangs around her like a cloud, there is worry in her deep brown eyes. She reminds me of a frightened bird, the way her eyes scan the room, apparently assessing her safety.

As a child, Sally had been a mother to her mother. When Sally was ten, her mother's second child was born. The serious complications for her mother from this birth developed into a two-year illness. Sally cared for the baby and for her mother. Whenever Sally wasn't immediately responsive to her mother's call, she heard, "You are so selfish." In order to avoid that damning label, Sally tried to be prepared for anything her mother might want at any time.

When she entered the convent after college, Sally taught grade school and then went into social work. She counseled homeless, abused women in a residential treatment center. Again, Sally was available to everyone most of the time. She was constantly exhausted but didn't consider taking time off. "No" was not in her vocabulary.

In her convent living situation, Sally was thrust into contact with many sisters. Being introverted by nature, Sally experienced this constant interaction as draining. She often felt frustrated and impatient with sisters who were inconsiderate of her needs for privacy or silence, but she took this to be a personal fault which she tried to overcome.

Life for Sally was a challenge in every arena. There was no place she could relax. She always felt pressured to "be nice." "I have everything I need to help people," she told me. "That's what I want to do with my life – make other people's lives easier." Part of the reason she was sitting in my office was that she wasn't performing up to her expectations for herself.

In our meetings, Sally was slow to trust. At our first session, she stated flatly, "I don't want to talk about my mother or my vocation." I honored her request but noted her two forbidden subjects. She told me about the frantic pace of her work days and the frustrations of her nights at the convent. If I were to offer any words of support recognizing her strain, she would brush me off defensively. Her back would straighten and she would assure me that "you don't understand," that nothing was wrong. I felt pushed away but I knew that acknowledging her own vulnerability was too threatening for Sally to handle.

Building a trusting relationship with me was painfully slow work but Sally would not consider terminating therapy. She was convinced there was something wrong with her that she needed to fix. She couldn't pinpoint what it was, but her experiences in close relationships had always led her to feel criticized and judged so she assumed something was amiss inside her.

Unconsciously, Sally expected me to treat her as poorly as other people had. Her fear showed in her habit of standing in the hall until I invited her to come into the office. She entered with her head and her eyes lowered. Often she wouldn't start speaking unless I asked her a question. When I didn't start the session for her, she would sit uncomfortably for several minutes as though she wanted to speak but felt compelled not to speak first. She had rules for herself which I didn't know.

One of her rules was that in any situation she had to comply. In our sessions, therefore, she thought that she had to let me set the tone. In the convent, she had to allow the other sisters to do what they wanted no matter how it affected her. At work, she had to take care of any needs the residents presented. She was alive simply to make others comfortable.

At times, when she would miss a session due to illness or during a session when she would complain of fatigue, I would try to explore with her what she could do to take care of her health. She seemed to view me as a heathen, trying to pull her away from serving God. Her suffering led her to feel like a good person. But I knew that at the base of her willingness to suffer was fear. It was only after I learned more about Sally's inner world figures that I understood her fear.

We talked about her life and then her feelings for months, not exploring any divergent approaches which would upset her preconception of therapy. As Sally realized the difference between thinking and feeling she acknowledged that her feelings didn't operate according to her intellect's rules. "I know I should help the elderly sisters at dinnertime, but I find them so unpleasant I don't even like being around them." She acknowledged that she wasn't the saint she tried to be.

We spoke in feeling words and defined her struggle between approval and integrity. Her Child's need for approval, which originated when she was very young but was never satisfactorily met, lingered. Since approval always comes from outside, any inner point of reference by which she could evaluate her own behavior and reward herself (thus leading to integrity) was not considered. But the approval was not satisfying or long lasting.

We focused on feeling her feelings as she spoke from them which lent immediacy to her experience. She wasn't talking about a thought or an ideal or even a feeling from the past. Her words sprang from the here-and-now flow in her body at the moment.

Sally realized that her inner world was dynamic. It moved and changed in response to a rhythm which was generated from deep within her and which was unconcerned with what her mind told her or what other people liked.

After Sally recognized the autonomous functioning of her inner world, we talked in terms of subpersonalities. The months of becoming acquainted with her inner world by watching her feelings change and move prepared Sally to accept the different parts of herself who had their own goals and needs.

With the diligence Sally employed to attack any task, she approached her inner world figures. Because she finally trusted me, she was willing to consider trusting her inner process, the dynamics among her subpersonalities. She listened, somewhat fearfully at first, hearing nothing for many weeks. But she would never give up on a task once she had accepted it, so regardless of the apparent lack of results, she persisted.

She focused her attention very precisely. She would start by breathing and letting her mind calm down from its continual busyness. Then she would let the dominant feeling in her develop and expand and fill her. She wouldn't fight it or try to analyze it; she would just allow it to be. By welcoming it and encouraging it to grow larger, Sally acknowledged the subpersonality carrying the feeling. With her acceptance, the subpersonality no longer maneuvered in a hidden, sneaky manner to avoid her conscious mind. Since Sally was willing to know her subpersonalities (as she had finally been willing to be known by me), they revealed themselves to her. (Subpersonalities are very sensitive little beings; if they think you don't want to know them, they won't intrude on your awareness. But they will continue to operate in your shadows.)

The first subpersonality who spoke to Sally was the Suffering Servant. After many minutes of listening attentively, some words became faintly audible:

Servant: You really should be helping others. It doesn't seem right for you to be sitting here, doing nothing. People need your efforts and your work.

Adult: I'm taking time to listen.

Servant: Listen to what? You know you should be giving others what they need. That's why you are on this earth.

Adult: So I have to produce work to justify my existence. Is that what you're saying?

Servant: We all do. Work now and your reward will come later.

Adult: I should work for a future reward? "Then" will be different from "now"?

Servant: If you work now and serve others you can make "then" be different. You have to earn salvation.

Adult: I have to <u>do</u> something in order to be saved?

Servant: Yes, work and help others and you will be rewarded.

Sally thanked the Suffering Servant and breathed and sat quietly. She allowed the Suffering Servant to speak to her and for three months this was the only voice she heard. She stayed in her Observer and didn't react to the Servant's words. Then, after one of the Servant's usual responses with Sally again thanking it and sitting quietly, she heard another voice. After hearing the words clearly, she could identify this voice as the Punitive Parent. It spoke to her:

Parent: You ought to be ashamed of yourself. Everyone else is working and you're loafing.

Adult: You want me to be different?

Parent: I want you to quit being selfish. You only think about what you want and how you feel. You're disgusting.

Adult: I feel guilty when I hear your words.

Parent: You should. If you were doing something productive, you'd feel better.

Staying in her Observer, Sally listened to the Punitive Parent tell her to be productive for another month before she responded:

Adult: Being productive doesn't take away unpleasant feelings.

With this subtle confrontation, Sally established that her Adult held her power, not the Parent who was so critical. By identifying with the Observer, she could hear the Parent without accepting the criticism. Then she could decide without emotion whose voice fit her. Before she was strongly anchored in her Observer, Sally could not discern the Parent's messages and, thus, they operated in her without her awareness.

Without any conscious decision, she noticed her responses to her Superiors changing, too. When she was in a position similar to the Child's with the inner Punitive Parent, i.e., being criticized and being treated as though she were powerless, she found herself responding in a self affirming way just as she did with her inner Parent. When a Superior would ask her to do more than she felt she could, she would decline. If she were called selfish or insensitive, she would respond that she was neither, but that she simply couldn't do any more. She didn't allow anyone outside or inside of her to demean her. When she stopped playing the role of Helpless Child to her inner authoritative Punitive Parent, she didn't assume that role with anyone in her external world, either.

Sally was pleased by these outer reflections of her inner work. She had affected her daily life experience by adjusting her consciousness; she no longer encountered external Punitive Parents when her internal Punitive Parent wasn't dominant. She began to grasp the connection between her inner identifications and her outer interpersonal experience. Her sense of personal power increased significantly.

As she continued her quiet periods of listening a masculine voice emerged – the Driver. After a few conversations with the Driver, his pattern became describable. He usually gave Sally a list of things to do:

Driver: If you start now you can finish the sewing and the book-keeping before supper and maybe get some letters written.

Adult: You always have things for me to do.

Driver: Just do the sewing, the bookkeeping, and the letters and then you can rest.

Adult: I don't trust you. You've told me that before, "Only these three things," and then I do them and I never rest more than a few minutes before you have another list.

Driver: Well, work fast and get everything done and then you can take all the time you want.

After a few weeks of observing him, Sally was well enough acquainted with the Driver to know that his list was endless. Any halt to the chores was temporary. He compiled a list of urgent jobs daily. Always there was the promise, "Just these three more things and then the pressure will be off," but Sally had heard that so many times with never a real break that she no longer trusted his promises. So, again, she followed her breath and waited. Sally practiced this exercise of breathing and listening daily. Often the dialogues were similar. Once in a while, she might hear from her Child or her Aching Body. But usually it was her Suffering Servant, Punitive Parent, or Driver subpersonality who spoke to her. By listening to them, Sally acknowledged their existence and their wants without identifying with them or acting them out.

She didn't jump up and do what the Suffering Servant, the Punitive Parent, or the Driver suggested. She listened to them and acknowledged them and followed her breathing. By doing this Sally learned that she was not equivalent to whomever her loudest subpersonality was at any given time. Just because she heard a voice forcefully did not mean that it was wise or working in her long-term best interest. She just noticed the voices and returned to her breathing.

She noticed that the voices softened and changed as she treated them respectfully but with caution. She didn't give any voice ultimate power. She didn't need approval from any particular subpersonality. When she owned her power by not letting her subpersonalities send her scurrying, she could maintain a sense of being "above the fray," as she termed it. She observed but didn't act.

By continuing this discipline, Sally became aware of deeper intuitions. Her more subtle voices – the Reflective Monk, the Poet, and the sensual Lover – had to be assured that Sally wanted to hear from them. She had to create an inner stillness and receptivity before they would speak to her. As she could do this frequently, she began to notice "quiet wisdom."

During Sally's silent moments, a re-evaluation of the meanings of responsibility and morality seemed to be occurring without her thinking mind being involved. She wrote in her journal:

> I've wanted so deeply to make the world better, to contribute to the good of the whole, to reduce suffering. I thought that I *should* do these things. That was what being a good Christian was about. I wanted to do my part. I've always felt frustrated, though, because I could never do enough. I would wear myself out working as hard as I could and still there would be poverty and suffering, not only in the world but in my neighborhood where I worked.

I'm not looking for fast results or even necessarily for tangible rewards, but have I really been doing anything other than just responding to those voices inside me which tell me to stay busy? Am I making myself sick for the sake of some neurotic subpersonality? I'm willing and eager to suffer if that will make the world better or if God wants it for some unseen purpose, but have I created a world, made up of some wacky characters who tell me rigid rules and then punish me so that in some convoluted way I can be right? Have I wanted to be right so much that I've organized a way to be right on my own? Have I made this whole thing up?

Am I keeping myself sick by following some rules that someone in my head thought up? What if God doesn't care if I work a lot? What if it's the Driver I'm trying to please and not God at all?

Is the Driver God's representative in my head? Or is the Driver a leftover from my mother who would punish me if I weren't busy? Am I making myself sick to keep my mother happy, when I don't even see her any more? Sometimes I feel so driven and I act so compulsively! I'm acting out of some old played-over-and-over tape which tells me to stay busy.

Am I creating God in my mother's image? Does God want the same thing from me that she did? She was always easier on me when I was sick, so being sick paid off. Does God want me to be sick? Is being good in my relationship with God the same as being good in the relationship with my mother? What does having a relationship with God mean?

In my other relationships, I don't figure out what relating to my friends means and then act that way forever and ever. I sit and talk and listen. Really, having relationships that are truly friendships has only happened in this last year. Before I was too busy doing something so I could avoid feeling guilty. I didn't value spending time with other people enough to have friendships develop. OK, so I have several friendships now. What does having a relationship with God mean?

Well, first I have to be open to know God. To get to know my friends I set aside time and I listen to them. When I was getting to know all the voices inside of me, I listened to them. Listening to God seems to be the first step in having a relationship. Who is He? Or is He She? When I think of God as She, I think of my mother and the Superiors in the convent. They have been Drivers. Can I separate God from them? I've been treating God as just another autocratic authority. I hate it when people generalize about me, thinking that they know me because they know I'm a sister. Knowing one thing about me doesn't let them know me. And knowing some other authority doesn't mean I know God.

So how do I get to know God? Listen. What do I listen to? The priest's Sunday sermons? Yuck! It's increasingly difficult for me to listen to other humans tell me what is right and how I'm bad and what I should do. I don't want to hear that from God.

In my own mind, I've made God in my mother's image. What if I've created God? Well, the good part about that is I can un-create Him. So, I want to listen without preconceived notions. What an interesting idea. Just listen.

When I stop and breathe and listen, I hear from all those other voices. Now, I know that none of them is God. They are just their own personalities. Just as God isn't the same as any person I've known, He is not the same as any of my subpersonalities. They have been formed as my reaction to other people or situations, or as my way of getting through some tight spots. Nothing eternal or wise about that. Just a way of getting by. God must be deeper and wiser than any of my other voices. I'll just sit and listen and when I hear other voices I can identify, I'll let them go. Then maybe I'll get deeper, closer to who God really is.

And so, Sally resumed her sitting and breathing and listening. Usually she would hear from one or more subpersonalities as she settled into a state of inner stillness. She allowed those voices to pass and she returned her attention to her breath.

After several months of doing this exercise of watching and breathing, Sally wrote:

My times alone, being still, are becoming more and more important to me. It's at those times I feel most alive, most connected with the world, most receptive to God's will. And my experience of God's will isn't like anything I've experienced with any human person. I don't hear a voice that says, "Do this and don't do that."

It's mostly just a "knowing" I have. Sometimes my hands tingle and I trust that God is telling me He's with me. Sometimes they don't and I don't have any manifestation of His presence except that I know everything's OK. "God's in His heaven and all's right with the world." I know all's not right with the world, but in another way, it is. I don't have to clean up messes and I don't have to make other people's lives turn out right and I don't have to make anyone happy.

In a way it sounds very selfish. (Isn't that funny? For me, finding God lay in embracing the quality which I was taught most to hate – selfishness.) It's selfish because I don't take it upon myself to change the world or even to show another person what truth really is. I just value so much those moments when I can be quiet and listen and be with God.

I enjoy my times with other people more. There seems to be a love which is larger than all of us which blankets us. We can move together or apart and still be covered by that love. And being covered by that love makes everything else less urgent. His love is with us all. So what are we working for? Not to earn acceptance; we already have it.

He's not asking me to fly around, knocking myself out. Now I can differentiate very well between the knowing I feel in His presence and my mind's injunctions to "do something."

Sometimes I feel the need to do something, but not out of desperation, it's not a struggle or a hope that this act will make me OK or safe. If I feel pulled to act, it's to do the act, not to earn a reward or make something else happen, but just to do whatever I feel called to do. And then I can let it go because I have no investment in how it turns out. I was just called to do it and so I do it and then I walk away and wait to be called again.

My life is much calmer; the peace is deeper than anything I've known. And it is all comes from listening inside. Beneath the voices, there is truth. The wisdom is in not being caught up in voices, in *not doing*. For me wisdom lies in my willingness to just be.

By listening and knowing her own subpersonalities, Sally was able to move beyond them into a realm that wasn't personal. In this deeper, transpersonal realm, her experience was not related to her past. It was an arena broader than her individual feelings. She realized the universality of human experience and felt her identification with the larger whole. She stopped viewing others in terms of their identification with their dominant subpersonalities. Since she could see beyond her own subpersonalities, she could also appreciate that there was a greater depth to others.

She experienced God by living at this level of connectedness. Her own identification with any one subpersonality previously had prevented that.

Sally had always been concerned with moral action, but after her therapy experience, she described morality as balancing the needs she heard from all of her subpersonalities, being willing to feel all of her feelings (not only the "acceptable" ones), and allowing her inner world to guide her. Spirituality was no longer separated from her body experience. It was not concerned with an ideal concept of how she thought she should be. Spirituality for Sally became living her bodily life responsibly and with commitment to her inner world. She placed authority for making decisions within herself and developed a new conscience. No longer was her conscience a set of rules someone older had taught her long ago. Now Sally experienced her conscience as her body experience which let her know when something she was doing or considering wasn't good for her. She valued her body as her seat of wisdom. She couldn't oppress its voice and use illness as a way to avoid knowing herself. By listening to her body and her inner world, Sally developed a strong sense of purpose on a daily and sometimes momentary basis.

EXERCISE

Spend several minutes doing the Relaxation exercise on page 9.

Let an image come to you symbolizing your body. (Pause) Let an image come to you symbolizing your mind. (Pause) Let an image come to you symbolizing your feelings. (Pause)

You stand at the base of a mountain with the three symbols that you have just imaged – your body, your mind, and your feelings. You are going to take them up the mountain. Have them join hands or connect in some other way. (Pause) Notice how they interact. (Pause) Walk up the mountain and notice how the journey proceeds. (Pause) What do you notice about each part of you? (Pause) Watch them move up the mountain. (Pause)

As you near the top of the mountain a habitat becomes apparent. Notice the details of this dwelling. (Pause) A Wise Person lives here and comes out now to speak to you and your body, mind, and feelings. (Pause) What do you notice about the Wise Person? (Pause) Notice the gender, the appearance, and the clothing of this Wise Person. (Pause) How does the Wise Person move? (Pause)

The Wise Person approaches your group, turns to your body, and gives it a message which offers guidance. Listen. (Pause) Then the Wise Person turns to your mind and delivers some words of guidance for that part. Listen. (Pause) Then the Wise Person speaks to your feelings. Listen. (Pause) Finally the Wise Person turns to you and offers you some advice. Listen. (Pause) If anyone wants to ask the Wise Person a question allow that to happen now. (Pause)

Each of the four of you thanks the Wise Person, turns, and begins the journey down the mountain. (Pause) Watch how this journey proceeds. (Pause) Notice how the parts interact with each other. (Pause) Notice if the walk is easy or difficult compared to the walk up the mountain. (Pause) Returning to the base of the mountain, all four of you touch or connect in some other way. (Pause) Watch. (Pause) Notice the relationships among the four of you now. (Pause) Say goodbye and follow your breathing.

What were the representations for you, your body, mind, and feelings? How did the four parts of you interact?

Describe the habitat at the top of the mountain. Describe the Wise Person.

What messages did the Wise Person give to the body, mind, feelings, and you? Describe the trip down the mountain.

When you reached the base of the mountain, what did you notice about the relationships among the body, mind, feelings, and you?

REFLECTIONS

Have you thought about responsibility as starting inside you?

What would being responsible to your inner world mean you would do?

Which subpersonality do you treat as a god—accepting its words unquestioningly?

How do you maintain a personal relationship with God, a Higher Power, or your Higher Self?

AFTERWORD

Knowing our unconscious is the most important work any of us can do. It's a challenge we're given as humans to allow what is hidden and mysterious inside us to emerge and evolve and guide us. The direction from the unconscious is precise and healing; we simply need to listen. By learning its language we can decipher its messages to us.

Subpersonalities speak from the unconscious. They change with time and experience so that the exercises you've done in these chapters can be repeated. You will have different experiences as your inner world moves.

When we commit to knowing our inner worlds we can't determine what we will hear. We can only listen. We let go of our preconceptions and say, "Whatever lives inside me right now I welcome." Then we wait passively and receive.

As you spend time with your subpersonalities, ask questions and listen. Allow the figures to talk to you. You may receive their messages in words, in images, in feelings, in intuitions, through another person's words, or by noticing the coincidences in your daily life. Your subpersonalities are your children. You allow them to heal by giving them your attention and being present to them. As they heal they bring you joy, peace, and vitality. Through them you experience a deep, wise aliveness that comes from your center and leads you beyond yourself.